After the Bloody Mary Game

After the Bloody Mary Game

Living into Humanism

David Breeden

Foreword by Amanda Poppei

WIPF & STOCK · Eugene, Oregon

AFTER THE BLOODY MARY GAME
Living into Humanism

Copyright © 2017 David Breeden. All rights reserved. Except for brief quotations in critical publications or reviews, no part of this book may be reproduced in any manner without prior written permission from the publisher. Write: Permissions, Wipf and Stock Publishers, 199 W. 8th Ave., Suite 3, Eugene, OR 97401.

Wipf & Stock
An Imprint of Wipf and Stock Publishers
199 W. 8th Ave., Suite 3
Eugene, OR 97401

www.wipfandstock.com

PAPERBACK ISBN: 978-1-5326-1328-9
HARDCOVER ISBN: 978-1-5326-1330-2
EBOOK ISBN: 978-1-5326-1329-6

Manufactured in the U.S.A.   JUNE 9, 2017

There ain't no answer. There ain't gonna be any answer. There never has been an answer. That's the answer.

—GERTRUDE STEIN

I am not a spectator watching this cataract, but a part of the water precipitated over the edge.

—GEORGE SANTAYANA

Contents

Foreword by Amanda Poppei | xi

How to Play the Bloody Mary Game | 1

1 Who Are These Humanists? | 3
  Stories, Stories | 5
  Off to See the Wizard | 6
  What's Your Universe Like? | 8
  Religion American Style (and the Church of Crazy) | 9
  The Myth of Science versus Religion | 11
  Moses, Jesus, Paul, and Sacred Soundbites | 14
  The Neighbors Are Zombies Living in Maslow's Basement! | 16
  Porous, Buffered, and the Search for Authenticity | 18
  Religion: It's Time for the Grown-Ups to Talk | 21
  The Open and Shut (?) Case on Religious Thinking and Cognitive Closure | 24
  Selma: Death of a Metanarrative | 26
  Lies, Noble Lies, and Big Lies | 28

2 What Do Humanists Believe? | 31
  What Are the Goals of Humanism? | 33
  Hate and Homo Sapiens | 34
  Roadmaps for the Soul (or: Hunting, Gathering, Singing) | 37
  A Semi-Private Idaho and Life in the Goldilocks Zone | 39
  Let's Agree to Agree on Subjectivity | 42
  Wounds and Healers | 45
  Tinfoil Hats and the Examined Life | 49

Humanism and Theology | 52
Reason Is Dead; Long Live . . . Advanced Hindsight | 54
Soapy Cilantro and Tasty Gods | 56
Subjectivity, Existence, and the Stories We Tell Ourselves | 58
Where Is the I in Me? | 61
B-liefs, A-liefs, and Seeing the Way Things Are | 64
White Privilege: "Kumbaya" Won't Cut It | 66
Beyond Mansplaining | 68
Seriously—Who Said We Can Choose Our Own Mysteries? | 73
Love Thy Neighbor as . . . | 77
Language, Love, and Capability | 80
Fallen Angels, Rising Apes, and the Knowledge of the Serpent | 83

3 Where Does Humanism Come From? | 87

Humanism, Like Mushrooms | 89
Three Decorating Ideas for the Mind (or Making Sense of Life) | 93
What Do Death Cults Really Want? | 95
Buffering for Fun and Profit | 97
Blinding and Beheading: One Path, Many Mountains | 100
Greenery without People: The Future of Post-Religious Community | 102
The Transient, the Permanent, and the Stitching Horse: Heresy and Razors | 104
What's in the Way Is the Way: Stoicism and the Spaces Between | 106

4 The Varieties of Humanism | 109

Religious Humanism: What Was Old Is New Again | 111
Humanism: A Way Forward | 114
Spiritual but Not . . . Keep Talking | 116
Congregational Humanist Liturgy: Creating a Religion-Neutral Zone | 120
The "Trinsics": Where Are You Comin' From? | 123
The Proof's in the Pudding (or What's Churchy about Church?) | 125
Nature, Nurture, Murder: The Lesson of Eugenics | 127
Building Better Primates | 131

The Spiritual Practice of Agnosticism | 133
Use Your Words, Earn Your Words | 136
Spiritual but Not Superstitious | 137
Woo without the Woo-Woo | 139
Why Does a Super-Nice Word Like "Spiritual" Make Humanists All Itchy? | 142
The Rise of the Totally Awesome "Whatever" God | 144
That's Why They Call It "Practice" | 146
You Might Be a Religious Naturalist | 148
Religion: It's What You Do | 156

5 **What's the Humanist Mission?** | 159
The Wrath of Pew | 160
Life, Liberty, and the Pursuit of ... What? | 162
Welcome to the Age of Practice | 169
Martian Sleeper Cells and the Spiritual Practice of Science | 171
Philosophers Know What They Need | 172
The Bigness of Our Littleness | 174
On Chopping Wood and Getting Unstuck | 176
The Olympics of a Reflective Life | 177
The Ol' Heave-Ho-Ho | 180
Going All Thoreau: Doing Social Justice | 182
Conscience and Choosing the Hill to Die On | 185
Eleanor Rigby's Selfie | 187
A Final Summary of Humanism: Who We Are, What We Do, Why It Matters | 189
Again Play the Bloody Mary Game | 192

Sources and Further Reading | 193
About the Author | 199

Foreword

MOST BOOKS ABOUT HUMANISM feel like a slog through a graduate-level philosophy text. Not this one.

In this little volume, the Rev. Dr. David Breeden invites us into something more akin to a kitchen table conversation. Starting with his own story and adding a big helping of imagination (zombies, anyone?), David introduces humanism in a way that makes it accessible and even fun. He certainly has the philosophical chops, and shows them, providing a great introduction to the history of humanism and the centuries of thinking behind it. But the overall feel is that of welcome, to all, to explore this way of thinking, this way of *being* together.

Which is no surprise. David's style as a minister is invitational and warm, and in many ways I believe it represents the future of humanism. No longer stuck behind dusty books or trapped in our over-intellectual heads, David invites the reader, the congregation he serves, and the wider world to experience humanism as it continues to evolve.

We need this evolution so sorely. Indeed, the world is calling out for a humanism that is embodied and alive, connected to the realities of our lives now. As we face racism, xenophobia, misogyny, and homophobia, we need a way of living that is connected to both our rational and emotional selves. I sometimes talk about the origin of the word "religion"—from the Latin *ligare*, "to bind together." If religion is what binds us back together, then humanism is a religion in truth. David makes the case for this and more in this work, and I commend it to you.

Rev. Amanda Poppei
Washington Ethical Society

How to Play the Bloody Mary Game

1. Go into a windowless bathroom and close the door.
2. Light a candle.
3. Turn off the electric light.
4. Turn on the water, hot or cold.
5. Spin around three times, saying, "I killed your baby, Mary Worth! I killed your baby, Mary Worth! I killed your baby, Mary Worth!"
6. Look into the mirror.
7. Run out the door screaming.

1

Who Are These Humanists?

> CULTURES ARE SHARED STORIES. Wars to end wars. Wars for independence from this or that. Civil wars. Why we have this value or that. Those who have other stories, stories differing from the norm, are suspect; they might be the other.
>
> —NEIL GAIMAN, *AMERICAN GODS*

Stories, Stories

People are storytellers. We tell stories to scare ourselves. We tell stories to embolden ourselves. We tell stories both to explain the obvious and to explain the inexplicable. We even tell stories just because we enjoy telling stories.

Just as storytelling, narrative, comes naturally to us, the need for narratives drives us.

Often, stories choose us: the tribe we are born into, the religion, the nation. All these provide ready-made stories that bind us into the social patterns of the tribe, religion, or nation.

Some of us never feel the need to examine or question these narratives. Some of us do.

The story of humanism is the story of a group of human beings—throughout human history and around the globe—who examined and questioned the foundational stories of their social and historical locations. Humanists continue to do that. As British humanist A. C. Grayling said, "humanism is an attitude."

It's an attitude of equanimity, compassion, reason, and wisdom.

Off to See the Wizard

Yes, we all have a story. We all have gotten to where we are now . . . somehow.

Who are we humanists? Born or made, humanists have played the Bloody Mary Game in one version or another or watched others playing it and . . . dared to consider the mirror long and hard. They have found, as poet and atheist Wallace Stevens said, the "nothing that is not there and the nothing that is."

Each of us has said, "There must be another way." That other way has something to do with reason and science and skepticism and learning and scholarship. Yet, each of us realizes that, as philosopher George Santayana put it, "I am not a spectator watching this cataract, but a part of the water precipitated over the edge."

We realize that in this life we must build the boat that keeps us afloat even as we sail it, for this is our one and only life. So, we tell a different story.

Since people are inventive animals who tell many stories, the existential question of who we are and what we should be doing in this life has been answered and continues to be answered in many ways. Some ways are dour. Some are fun. Some are for profit. Some are for fun. Some work well; others don't.

Many books promise a secret—a powerful cure to what ails the human mind. This book only offers some notes toward working it out yourself.

Here's what I can say of humanism: no promises. But no superstition, either. Nothing but . . . a way that won't assault the conscience or the intelligence.

That said, humanists do not start from the premise that we have the only answer. It is only that most humanists long to know "reality" in as close an approximation to what is real as is humanly possible. No games.

Yes, such a stance requires a great deal of skepticism, but belief that we have found the one true and eternal way implies an answer, and an answer implies the cessation of exploration. Stopping our inquiry is not part of the humanist way, just as stopping the search is not the scientific method. One answer merely opens a door to many others.

Who Are These Humanists?

Humanism asserts that inertia is not a value system. Inertia is what slows an object down. Inertia brings an object to a stop. Humanists do not stop.

A vibrant value system moves us off dead center. A vibrant value system motivates. Inertia is surface, superficial. Humanists demand depth. We wish to live broadly and deeply as we crash over that precipice.

Humanists are edgy people.

What's Your Universe Like?

As a start, here are some definitions:

> Humanism is an evidence-based value system dedicated to freedom of thought and the promotion of the well-being of the planet and living things.

Humanists tend to be naturalists:

> Naturalism proposes that only measurable materials and forces make up the cosmos.

What is religion?

> Religion is a method by which human beings discover priorities and commit (and recommit) to acting on them. (The first Humanist Manifesto defined "religion" as "those actions, purposes, and experiences which are humanly significant").

At its essence, the feeling that is often defined as "religious" is about how the perceived self (which science tells us doesn't actually exist) meshes with the universe, the Big Other (which isn't other and shouldn't feel that way but does).

Add "religious" to "naturalism" and you get: religious naturalism. Definition:

> Religious Naturalism is religious practice without reference to supernaturalism. There is no mind/body or flesh/spirit dichotomy. The focus is on the universe and our part in it.

Stoic philosopher Marcus Aurelius perhaps best stated the task:

> Always keep in mind the nature of the universe and the nature or your own nature and how the one relates to the other and what being a part of the entire universe means. Remember that no one can stop you from doing and saying those things which are your part in the universe.[1]

1. *Meditations*, II.9 (author's translation).

Religion American Style (and the Church of Crazy)

Let's face it, the United States has produced some way-crazy religions. Not to name any names, but anybody can name names . . . way crazy.

Sometimes, when I hear from some of the progeny of those way-crazy religions, I have to wish that the Reformation hadn't happened and the pope could still pull a switch and put a stop to the crazy. Where's the Vatican army when Alabama needs it?

But that's just not how the United States of America operates. The US and crazy religions are like Sonny and Cher. Or U and 2. And, well, the beat goes on. That's what the latest Pew poll on religious affiliation shows— Americans are striking out for the spiritual territories. And the next poll will show that too. And the next. (I've gone from Pentecostal to humanist Unitarian—and a few things in between—in my life. And I ain't done yet.)

Let's face it: it takes individualism to make it in the US. I'm not talking about "making it" in social capital terms. I'm talking about scratching out a living in the "richest nation on Earth" where most of us are poor. Want to become an existentialist? Try getting your car repossessed.

From the very beginning of the European invasion, this nation has produced DIY religious crazies—heck, the Puritans were "nones," people!

And the Quakers. And . . .

The United States is the Home Depot of Religion. Gimme some power tools and a video, and I'll build that sucker. Ask Joseph Smith.

The American pretense toward "everybody is middle-class" that took hold in the 1960s held sway a little while, and mainline religion appeared to be sitting in the catbird seat. But that middle-class pretense went the way of the union and the dream of a social safety net.

The US is a land where Jesus speaks to anyone who will listen (or let's say that anyone so inclined can hear Jesus). There's no need for the Vatican. Jesus talks in the sort of trailer parks I grew up in. Jesus stalks Walmart, where Bibles, prophylactics, semiautomatic weapons, and whiskey are only a bounced check away. (I know a guy who did this, and he praised the Lord when they took the check.)

The rise of the "nones"—the unchurched DIY followers of Jesus, Buddha, Patanjali, and any number of other charismatic figures (or, what the hey, all of the above)—neither spells doom for Christian orthodoxy nor presages the rise of the rational secular hordes. It's merely the DIY impulse that brought you the First, Second, and Third Great Awakenings. Welcome to the Fourth. And the Age of Aquarius and the Second or Third Coming, for that matter.

We Americans are crazy. We have to be to sustain an illusion as large as ours. Still and all, we know a good deal when we see one. At the pawn shop. On the street corner. Or at the church on TV. We will take that deal, thank you very much. We will take that tune and sing it ourselves.

So the "nones" are a quarter of the US population now? The only change is that they're just not putting any shade on their act.

Put this in your pipe and smoke it: on one of his US visits, Pope John Paul II was horrified when American Catholics took the host from his hand and fed it to themselves. Heresy? Welcome to America, pal.

From humanism to Scientology, it's all about DIY.

Do it yourself, baby. For good or ill, that's religion American style.

The Myth of Science versus Religion

It was the German writer Heinrich Heine who imagined a battle between the Hebrews and Hellenes. Soon that battle came to be imagined as Jerusalem versus Athens. Nowadays, we endlessly tease at the science/religion chasm. Endlessly we ask: Is it a chasm? A great divide? Are the two reconcilable?

Heine was looking to his recent European past, what we nowadays call the Age of Enlightenment, in which the chief theorists had seen themselves as purveyors of light to a world darkened by religion. Diderot. Voltaire. Hume. As Diderot put it, "We preach wisdom to the deaf, and we are still far indeed from the age of reason."

The Enlightenment thinkers created a narrative in which the ancient world—by which they meant Classical Greece and Rome—had risen to great heights of human achievement only to fall before the juggernaut of Christianity. The Italian poet and scholar Petrarch first named that period of Christianity's rise the "Dark Ages."

"Enlightenment" was the antidote. This time, Reason would not fail . . .

This narrative has continued. Heine himself is remembered as a Romantic, throwing off the shackles of Reason to get in touch again with the human heart. With the US version of Romanticism—transcendentalism—Ralph Waldo Emerson saw himself battling against the cold reason that had descended upon the Unitarian thinking of his time.

Building on this tradition, the first Humanist Manifesto of 1933 began explicitly: "The time is past for mere revision of traditional attitudes." Both humanists and their opponents saw humanism as a radical departure from religious tradition, an alternative to traditional religion that would one day defeat superstition. That departure from Western thought was more apparent than real, however.

For one thing, the concept of a god disassociated from, and above, nature—a concept born of the agricultural revolution and its resultant extreme hierarchies—was actually a radical departure from older human understandings of deities that existed as part of nature itself.

The idea of a personal god—growing today among Christians—and the idea of nature itself as the sacred are the older understandings—it's back to the future.

The modernist ideology of the early twentieth century insisted that a new age required new—and decisively disjunctive—thinking. This was true, modernists insisted, as much in humanism as in twelve-tone musical composition or Cubist painting. With the clear vision of hindsight, however, we can easily see that the modernist impulse was very much a part of the cultures in which such aesthetics developed. And those aesthetics became part of the vocabulary of the arts to come. Just so humanism.

Just as the artists and writers of the modernist epoch issued manifestos to establish and promote their new art movements, humanists proudly declared their independence from convention and the past. We do well to suspect their exuberance, however.

Yet the "battle" goes on. If in doubt, do a Web search on "science verses religion"—court cases, polemics, politicians, fuss and bother.

The "battle" is good for headlines and now "clickbait," but the battle of good and evil, light and darkness, that Petrarch and his grandchildren of the Enlightenment delineated is about politics, not philosophy or religion.

As a humanist myself, I'm placed willy-nilly in a camp. I don't think there are any camps, however. For Enlightenment philosopher David Hume, a heresy trial and the gallows were real possibilities. In some parts of our planet, similar consequences still await. But, again, that's politics, not religion and philosophy meeting in conversation.

In those places in the world where freedom of—and from—religion exists, most people choose to visit a physician when they have physical ailments. Most people go to auto mechanics rather than saying prayers over broken cars. We may chat and pray with chaplains about suffering and death and dying, but we trust to physicians and psychologists when the rubber meets the road.

In that world, humanism and a materialist world view do not stand in stark contrast or in opposition to religions, but as the non-metaphorical alternative, using "day language" as opposed to "night language," as Michael Dowd, the evangelist of evolution, puts it. Yes, that's still a light/dark metaphor, but not one of warfare. Merely the ebb and flow of human thinking from one metaphor and frame to another on any given day.

The Enlightenment and its child, humanism, were not discontinuous from their pasts but part of the evolution of human thought. As a humanist,

I see religions of all stripes not as containers for truths but as interesting literature, interesting culture, and fascinating antique shops for wandering through, picking up the odd spinning wheel or cowbell. They are old interpretive systems that sought for answers that scholarship and science now answer in much more useful and effective ways. Still, late at night, there is that sudden noise . . .

Yes, religion, like scientific thinking, continues to evolve. Yet it's time to see something clearly: the "science versus religion" paradigm puts religion in a place it has no business being. Yes, in many places and cultures religions oppose science, but that does not mean that religions hold opposing truths—only that ignorant people have taken unwarranted power.

As the German philosopher Emmanuel Kant put it: "We live not in an enlightened age but an Age of Enlightenment." And so it goes.

Moses, Jesus, Paul, and Sacred Soundbites

"Use your own little head." That's a phrase I learned from my fundamentalist Christian mother: "Use your own little head."

By it, she meant for teenage me to "listen to my raisin"—another catchphrase—rather than to my peers. My mother was cautioning me to use my own head. Further, at least to my future-humanist ears, she was saying that reason, not my gut, should determine my actions.

Nowadays I ask, "Shouldn't reason, not the religions of our various cultural backgrounds, serve as the arbiter of public discourse and our efforts at realizing a just society?"

As a multifaith leader, I spend a lot of time saying and showing that people of diverse religious faiths can find common ground. I believe in that work.

I'm also convinced that our common evolution as cooperative and rational animals trumps the overlays of religion and culture made since our common trek from the Rift Valley.

We are rational animals. After all, which would you prefer for a physician: someone who feels your pain, or someone who knows how to stop your pain? Listening to the heart is a fine thing to do. And, there's no doubt that scriptures often provide great sound bites.

Listening to our own heads is the hard part. Using Moses, Jesus, Paul et al. as motivators and guides is great. But they are not living in our time and circumstance.

As he watched the bloody carnage justified on both sides by Christian theology, Abraham Lincoln perhaps said it best:

> I know that the Lord is always on the side of the right. But it is my constant anxiety and prayer that I and this nation should be on the Lord's side.

Which side is the Lord's side? Or is it that God plays for both teams? Or is it that human beings are condemned to action that may or may not be "right" until God (or Satan?) sorts it out?

This contrast came home to me during the fight over gay marriage in the state of Minnesota, where I live. Progressive religious leaders took a long look at the reign of the Religious Right in politics and decided to counter it. We took the Christian message of love and inclusion to the statehouse. I knew that we had accomplished the goal when a conservative state senator said, "This is about more than religion."

The worm had turned. And, indeed, the right to marry became law in the state of Minnesota.

Many of my religious colleagues believe that the loving and inclusive message of their faith traditions prevailed. Don't get me wrong—I'm all for loving and inclusion. It's the cherry-picking of the messages of Moses, Jesus, Paul et al. that bothers me a bit.

Weren't we progressives cherry-picking and sound-biting as crassly as our conservative opponents?

Where were the real Moses and Jesus and Paul in all this?

Perhaps our hearts were telling us things. Perhaps our sense of right and wrong was talking, on both sides. But these sacred thinkers weren't saying anything new—anything that the scriptures weren't telling Abe Lincoln and Jeff Davis back in their days of choosing whom to slaughter and why based on those same old writings.

This gives me pause. As we make decisions in the twenty-first century, are we best served by referring to old texts and deities that have not done a whole lot of clear talking? Perhaps it's time to use our own little heads.

The Neighbors Are Zombies Living in Maslow's Basement!

Imagine the laid-back life of a zombie.

First of all, you're dead. So. No more taxes. That's for sure. And those pesky monthly bills will bother you no more.

Besides no more worries about death and taxes, look at how focused you are: your meaning and purpose have boiled down to searching for brains to eat. That's focused.

And zombies have lots of friends.

Being undead has its moments. You're well beyond all the "slings and arrows of outrageous fortune." Your only worry is getting shot in the head.

Director George A. Romero, who directed *Night of the Living Dead*, is credited with having created the contemporary zombie. He has this to say: "I just took some of the *mysterioso* stuff of voodoo out of it, and made them the neighbors. Neighbors are frightening enough when they're alive."

I have a suspicion this goes a long way toward explaining the huge popularity of zombies. Perhaps they represent all the danger we see in others and in ourselves.

Chip and Dan Heath, marketing gurus, have come up with the term "Maslow's Basement." Their argument is that most marketing depends upon the bottom end of psychologist Abraham Maslow's "hierarch of needs" pyramid. In that model, there are three principles that motivate people to buy a product: fear, greed, or lust. These are base desires, Maslow's Basement.

I suppose the high end of Maslow's hierarchy, such things as morality, creativity, and spontaneity, is Maslow's Attic. (Zombies definitely live in the basement.)

Research shows that people see others as motivated by fear, greed, and lust.[1] But people self-report that their actions are motivated by empathy and compassion. In other words, we fear their neighbors, just as director George A. Romero claims.

---

1. This is the sinister attribution error: paranoid cognition and collective distrust in groups and organizations. See Kramer, "Motivation and Emotion."

The counterintuitive fact may be that the self-reporting is correct. Meaning that all of us—including our neighbors—are more influenced by compassion and empathy than by Maslow's Basement motivators of fear, greed, and lust.

We may be selling our species short! Perhaps our default mode is *not* to dwell in Maslow's Basement. Perhaps our neighbors are not potential zombies.

Perhaps we all, as Oscar Wilde said, despite having our feet in the gutter, are looking at the stars.

The zombie apocalypse will not be televised. Because it's not coming. Because most of us are inclined to treat our neighbors . . . not as zombies but as ourselves.

If only we can figure out how to sell that . . .

Porous, Buffered, and the Search for Authenticity

From the First Great Awakening of the 1740s which energized the North American colonists and eventually led to the American Revolution, to the transcendentalists to the Beats, Hippies, and What-Have-Yous, a frequent cry of Americans has been "authenticity." Americans want it to be real, genuine, visceral, heartfelt, rough-hewn . . . something like that.

Authenticity, I take it, has something to do with being yourself. Or finding yourself. Or getting out of your head and into your heart. Something like that.

In the US, finding one's authentic self has often involved hitting the open road and going West. Or heading to the big city. Sometimes it's the distance from the pew to the alter in a Holy Roller church. Or to the free air of an ashram after escape from the stale breath of a parish church.

It often involves both geographic space and psychic distance—the distance from of a Midwestern farm to Gay Paree, or from Hometown, USA to Greenwich Village or North Beach.

Whatever else it might be, it appears that the authentic self is open to new experience and fresh possibility. A self that is open to taking advantage of options. And changing fundamental beliefs. (It is also a marketing opportunity. The authentic individual often needs a particular look and particular accoutrements which the market can supply.)

I grew up in a farming community near the Ohio River. For transportation, my parents rode farm wagons pulled by horses into the nearest town when they were kids. For children of the farm and the Depression, after the war, the speed and power of a 185-horsepower V-8 Chevrolet engine on a paved road spoke to them of possibility and adventure.

My parents transformed themselves from farmers to factory workers. The sort of folks the Beats, also of their generation, found square. Authenticity, it appears, comes in many packages.

My father was born prematurely in a two-room sharecropper's shack. He survived because August without air conditioning is a great incubator. His family nearly starved during the Depression. Next, he survived

Who Are These Humanists?

house-to-house and hand-to-hand combat in Europe during the Second World War. Then he worked as a boilermaker, sometimes suspended high over the water, working on ships; sometimes he worked several stories up, on smoke stacks.

My farmer parents were what philosopher Charles Taylor termed "porous selves." They lived fully aware of the difficulty and dangers of survival. This reinforced their faith in the Christianity of the lower Ohio River Valley.

My parents were the sort of people for whom life itself is as authentic and real as anybody can want. "The real" came to them. They weren't out looking for authenticity . . . nor did they seek new religious thinking.

As Charles Taylor puts it, "the porous self is vulnerable, to spirits, demons, cosmic forces. And along with this go certain fears which can grip it in certain circumstances. The buffered self has been taken out of the world of this kind of fear."[1]

This "buffered self," according to Taylor, often becomes secular, or at least "believes" in received religions only insofar as this self chooses not to seek authenticity in that direction. Buffered people are free enough, in other words, from the fear of looming, immanent privation and death to—if they choose—begin examining cultural assumptions, including their religious ideas.

Psychologist Abraham Maslow had a similar idea, which he called a "hierarchy of needs."

A very large shift in US consciousness occurred after World War II. Many Americans—like me—were able to move from a porous understanding to buffered understanding. Beat writers such as Jack Kerouac or Allan Ginsberg or Gregory Corso became models for the religious, spiritual, and artistic quests of Boomers such as I.

Remember what Charles Taylor said: "The buffered self has been taken out of the world . . . of fear." Unlike my parents, I never faced starvation. Or war. Or educational deprivation. Or the feeling of being less-than because of my social location in US society.

Charles Taylor's distinction helps clarify why safety leads to secularity. Why it is that people who are not in constant want and fear choose to drop out of their childhood religions and question the norms they have been taught. And it may be there's no going back. Immediately after the September 11th attacks, the churches and synagogues and mosques of the America were full. My supposition at the time was that the fear of the day

---

1. Taylor, *Secular Age*, 38.

would lead to a resurgence of piety of the sort that swept the nation during the Red Scare of the 1950s.

This did not happen.

As a matter of fact, the reverse has been true—attendance has dropped steadily ever since. It appears Americans felt "porous" for a short time but returned to "buffered" robustly, despite the media's focus on threats. Why?

Perhaps it's relatively easy to feel safe in the US of the twenty-first century, despite constant bombings and shootings and low-level wars and rising debt and poverty. Perhaps most Americans still feel that the likelihood of growing old is in our favor. Perhaps it's always 9/11 now. But we have adjusted to that new normal.

After all, that "invisible hand" of capitalism continues to pump out the calories and the iPhones. We go on, wandering from one religion to another, one answer to another. We go on seeking authenticity.

Whatever that means.

Religion: It's Time for the Grown-Ups to Talk

In November of 1726 news reached London that a physician had assisted a woman named Mary Tofts as she gave birth to . . . a rabbit.

The rabbit, unfortunately, died.

Mary Tofts got quite a lot of attention at the time. And even more attention when she gave birth to yet another rabbit—or, well, at least rabbit parts. And then another. With various physicians in attendance.

All the rabbits died, but all the physicians who were called in to assist the births swore that Mary Tofts had indeed given birth to rabbits, albeit dead ones or bits of ones.

This continued for some time, and Mary gained great notoriety.

The curious fate of Mary Tofts "proved" a theory of the time. This was a theory that in the day was taken quite seriously called "maternal impression." Pregnant women were warned to be careful what they looked at, lest they get an impression of an animal, and their babies be born resembling various animals.

Tofts's case appeared to prove this theory. Mary claimed to have seen a rabbit just before she went into labor. Her case reinforced a theory.

Eventually, a skeptical physician did some investigating and discovered that Mary's husband had been purchasing large numbers of baby rabbits . . . Which got the skeptic to thinking: Why had Mary Tofts . . . ahem . . . "conceived" of this deception? Because she had been told that being famous would . . . make her money . . .

A theory—that of "maternal impression"—gave . . . ahem . . . birth . . . to Mary Tofts and her rabbit deliveries.

The case might perhaps be a lesson to us: sometimes our theories go in search of proof. Observation bias, observer-expectancy effect. We know that experiment too often proves the assumptions researchers suspected when they began.

Confession: I want to know, as closely as I can, what is true—what is really there. I don't want my trite, parochial prejudices to affect my search for truth and meaning. I don't want to believe that women give birth to rabbits or that dinosaurs and human beings existed at the same time.

I want this, knowing full well that at one time as close as I could have gotten to "real" or "true" would have told me that the Mediterranean Sea is the center of the Earth. That at another time the closest I could have gotten to reality was that the sun is the center of the universe. Later, that the universe was static. Then, that the universe was expanding at a constant rate. Now, that there's dark matter. And on. And on.

I know that "as close as" one can get to the real is not all that close, ever. I also know that the latest and best scientific and scholarly knowledge is as close to real as the human mind is going to get . . .

In *Gulliver's Travels* Jonathan Swift tells the story of the endless war between the Big-Endians and the Little-Endians. The Little-Endians break their boiled eggs at the small end. The Big-Endians break theirs at the big end. Swift reports that one king lost his crown and another lost his life due to this war. Swift had the battle between the Roman Catholic and Protestant views of the Eucharist in mind. A dispute that continues to this day and has cost the lives of millions.

Silly, Jonathan Swift was saying. How silly and childish.

Yet it seems that both Swift's characters and we human beings will take just about any excuse to create tribes and cliques and circles and insiders and outsiders.

Let's be real: anyone who accepts the scientific method as an arbiter of truth is a humanist (little "h"). Some who accept the scientific method reserve a bit to be kept for the mysterious or even the supernatural; some don't.

Some of us don't think there is any "super" before the natural; some of us leave room for doubt.

The shambles that is our world as it is—governed as it is by various conceptions of gods—argues against the efficacy of fighting over such things, doesn't it?

The Crusades? The Holy Roman Empire? Victorian London? La Belle Epoch? When was it that god was "in his heaven and all right with the world," as Robert Browning famously said?

Fighting about such things didn't work in the "good old days" (whenever that might have been) and doesn't work now. It's time that the Little-Endians and the Big-Endians chill out and realize it's just a friggin' egg.

In matters of religion, the question of who is right and who wrong dims before the fact that so many people are harmed by the wrangling and tribalism around the question.

It's just an egg.

Who will be the grown-ups?

What is the practical difference in actions between atheists, agnostics, theists and those who just don't care?

People of whatever denominational stripe who believe in science, in the separation of church and state, and in the education of children to be critical thinkers—progressive people—have a lot in common, no matter which end of the boiled egg they break.

It's time those people act like grown-ups.

The Open and Shut (?) Case on Religious Thinking and Cognitive Closure

It isn't news that there's an inverse relation between religious fundamentalism and social innovation. Religion is a handbrake; whether it stops humanity from going uphill or downhill is the only question.

When a new study comes out telling us what we already know about secularity, my secular acquaintances do the "I told you so" as fundamentalists squint and look for flaws in the statistics.

The latest study, Roland Bénabou and colleagues' "Forbidden Fruits: The Political Economy of Science, Religion, and Growth," is the most thorough study yet. Furthermore, it hits in the pocketbook: religion costs the economy.

Not to ruin the study's punch line, but both internationally and in the US the secular spots are the innovative spots. And vice versa. In the US, religiosity drags down innovation in all but two of the old Confederate States of America.

What's up with this?

OK, I'm a humanist. Most humanists don't put much credence in the revelations of the various scriptures and traditions of religions. Many of us are agnostic or atheist. We tend to put our trust in reason, scholarship, and the scientific method, ways of thinking predicated on not knowing. We like mystery, because it gives us something to do on long afternoons. We like not knowing what we don't know and knowing we don't know much.

According to this latest study, the humanist brain is a good place to be if you happen to be an innovative idea. Why? Dr. Arie Kruglanski, a social psychologist, has created the theory of "cognitive closure." His theory examines the fact that some people are more comfortable with ambiguity than others. Humanists eat ambiguity for breakfast. We love it. But some folks search for a definitive answer, even if that answer is . . . well, clearly wrong . . . an answer with flaws even the believer can see (but chooses to ignore or compartmentalize).

That's why Dr. Kruglanski gets the call when we try to understand the minds of terrorists. Some of us don't need closure all that much. But many of us do—whatever the cost to our own reasoning abilities.

Yet, yet, but . . . the question that generated the US portion of the study was this: "Are you a religious person, not a religious person, a convinced atheist, or don't know?"

Those who identify themselves with their (mainline) religions as a primary descriptor will clearly pick "religious person." But what about those who identify as pagan? Buddhist? Spiritual but not religious? Unitarian Universalists . . .

I happened to grow up in a fundamentalist tradition that absolutely required cognitive closure—the sort of folks who build creationist museums. Yet, as an agnostic humanist, I also would tick the box for "religious person." I think a lot about my values and actions and I work hard to live out my values. To me, that's a religious person.

Yes, there is value in the mounting heap of studies that indicate that religion can be bad for society. But, dear researchers, please avoid cognitive closure! Some of us are spiritual but not religious, and some of us are religious but humanist, drinking ambiguity like an ever-flowing stream.

Complexity. It's what makes science, science.

Selma: Death of a Metanarrative

OK, I admit it—I love it when postmodernism calls it right. And the screeches and whines that have emanated over media since the film appeared are the sound of metanarratives dying.

It was the French philosopher Jean-François Lyotard who postulated that the essence of postmodernism is "incredulity toward metanarratives."

A metanarrative is a big overarching myth (lie) that justifies the ways of power to man (and woman). One metanarrative is that the Europeans who journeyed to the Western Hemisphere were up to good rather than no-good. Another metanarrative is that hopeful bit of liberal thought that says "the arc of the universe bends toward justice." Another metanarrative is that the US has a constitutional government that has some flaws but will—given time and patience—eventually work out for everyone. Yes, the music swells at a happy ending . . .

Sure, postmodernism itself is a metanarrative; and it has led to some atrocities of prose, but thinkers such as Leotard have given us a way of looking at the Big Lies that drive power structures. An old African proverb says it better than 99 percent of postmodernist writing: "Until lions have historians, tales of the hunt will glorify the hunter."

Director Ava DuVernay (Paul Webb shares the writing credit) has some incredulity going on, and her film blows apart several sacred metanarratives. One metanarrative is that the "good" federal government swept in and curtailed the power of "bad" state government. Another is that White liberals played a starring role in the struggle. Another is that Black men led the struggle. Finally, the lions have a historian.

Art doesn't pretend to be "true," if by "truth" we mean following the scripts written to build a metanarrative. DuVernay has created a truer true.

I grew up in the South (poor and White) not too far from Selma. I remember those days. The terrorists were the locals. The heroes were not (as much) those who swept in on jets in front of cameras but the ones who acted for justice knowing full well that the Klan knew where they lived—and believe me, it gets very dark in the rural South.

That's the story Ava DeVernay tells. It's not an easy story to tell in a couple of hours or in the face of metanarraatives or in the shadow of a very real titan such as Martin Luther King Jr.

But it's how justice gets done in the real world.

Lies, Noble Lies, and Big Lies

The "noble lie." Plato first wrote about it in *The Republic*. According to Plato, a noble lie is absurd to those who think about it, but serves as the base—the foundation—of a social structure. A Noble Lie justifies the way things are to the masses in order for the ruling elite to remain the ruling elite.

Plato proposes the Noble Lie in the context of Socrates discussing the nature of democracy, in which the free play of ideas is assumed.

Socrates proposes two Noble Lies: One, citizens are to be told that human beings are born not from human parents but from the Earth itself. And two, that each person, upon birth, has a bit of metal inside her or his soul: the aristocrats gold, the soldiers and traders silver, and the peasants iron.

Plato knew that these propositions are absurd, but he uses the absurdity of the propositions to point out that foundational lies keep social structures stable. If, Socrates says, citizens believe they are of the Earth, they will be more willing to die for their country and less likely to adhere to family and clan connections. As to the second Noble Lie, it serves to keep people in their social classes: those born with iron in their souls will accept that they have no business trying to become part of the ruling elite.

Plato is making the point that societies necessarily have Noble Lies at their foundations, though these lies are most likely not so well crafted to the purposes they wish to serve as the ones that Socrates proposes.

In this telling of the issue, there are no "Noble Truths," because nothing can hold up to that kind of pressure and scrutiny. There's only one truth of government, I think Plato is saying, and that is to perpetuate the advantages of those who are in power.

What are the Noble Lies of the United States, and who came up with them?

Nations that allow the free play of ideas will have competing Noble Lies.

Who Are These Humanists?

Plato would be the first one to tell us that we choose the Noble Lies that we embrace according to our preexisting prejudices. Then, most of us even believe those lies are the truth.

The Noble Lies that we don't agree with we call "Big Lies."

"Big Lies" is a concept from Adolf Hitler's *Mein Kampf*. Hitler said, "The masses of the people . . . will more easily fall victim to a big lie than to a small one." As Hitler knew, the best way to perpetrate a Big Lie is to tell one that appeals to the preexisting prejudices of people. Thus, Hitler insisted that Germany's problems were the result of actions by Jews. That was a Big Lie.

Hitler got away with it for some years and did a great deal of damage with it. In the 1950s, Joseph McCarthy told the Big Lie that the State Department was full of Communists. After he was successful with that Big Lie, he told an even bigger lie. Unfortunately, his Big Lie led to the purge of everyone in the State Department who knew anything about Vietnam and the problems there. Which led to a national disaster.

That's the way I see it. But what is and what isn't a Big Lie . . . to a great extent lies in the eyes of the beholder.

For me, for example, it's a Big Lie that the "invisible hand of the market" will create a just and equitable economic system. For those on the other side of the argument, it's a Big Lie that government can intervene positively in a free market economy.

Who's lying? Well, that's a problem, isn't it? Plato is there to say that both sides are lying, because both sides are using the Big Lies—which we consider Noble Lies or perhaps even the truth—to achieve what we see as desirable ends.

I believe it to be a truth that spreading the wealth around to more people is a positive good; others believe that the accumulation of wealth is the only way to encourage innovation and progress. Sure, believing that everyone is a little bit right probably is closer to the truth of the matter. But that doesn't make for robust politics and debate, does it?

Thus, according to Plato, embracing a Noble Lie on one extreme or the other is the best way to promote the kind of free interchange of ideas that leads to democracy.

The big lie. The noble lie. They are lies told because we believe so deeply and strongly that they will get us to truth.

But, Plato tells us, here's the thing: they don't!

They remain big—and not so noble—lies. They are practices to deceive by people who are themselves deceived (unless perhaps they become philosophers).

And remember, in Plato's view, we are supposed to be living examined lives that will result in our knowing the true truth . . .

Are religions Noble Lies or Big Lies?

2

What Do Humanists Believe?

THE TRUE MYSTERY OF the world is the visible, not the invisible.

—OSCAR WILDE

What Are the Goals of Humanism?

- To grow beyond damaging tribalisms, whether of religion, race, gender, nation, location, class, or any of the other boundaries chosen to do damage.
- To grow beyond patriarchy.
- To encourage human potential and the diversity of human expression, in art, in life.
- To pursue knowledge and wisdom, wherever the pursuit leads.
- To implement the United Nations Universal Declaration of Human Rights and to strengthen the United Nations.
- To end economic inequality.
- To care for the planet and its biological diversity.
- To help all of humanity move beyond . . .

*These goals are both individual and communal.

Hate and *Homo Sapiens*

Had space aliens stopped by planet Earth a hundred thousand years ago, as *Homo sapiens* first began to migrate north out of Africa, I suspect they would have noted in their star log that these evolving creatures had a very serious challenge before them: divisive tribalism.

Yes, the aliens would have noted, *Homo sapiens* is remarkable at invention. Remarkable at problem solving. Highly adaptable to new climates and new food sources. Very affectionate and respectful and loyal within family and tribal groups.

Yet, when it comes to one tribe interacting with another, one group understanding another, there is often trouble. No, usually trouble. Trouble to the point of armed violence and slaughter.

Those aliens might very well have filed in their star log that *Homo sapiens* might survive—and even thrive—were they able to get past the ill effects of their ability to find the smallest differences . . . and make a big deal out of each and every one.

What do we want in a tribe? Unfortunately, it appears that our default setting is to want everyone to look, think, act, and be . . . exactly as we are.

That's why it is still true, as Martin Luther King Jr. said long ago, that Sunday morning is the most segregated time in America. Only 8 percent of US congregations are integrated in any meaningful way. Eight percent. After all those years of trying. And, let's face it, mainline Protestant denominations, such as Episcopalians and Presbyterians and Unitarian Universalists, have really, really tried.

Why divisive tribalism?

Psychologist Gordon Allport isn't much known these days—he died in 1967—but when it comes to the study of good ol' human tribalism, we parrot his work constantly.

Allport set out to examine how our attitudes and prejudices are constantly evolving. It would at first appear that getting to know people of other races and cultures is a no-brainer in terms of reducing prejudices. But it turns out this is not as simple as it seems.

For example, in the southern United States, Blacks and Whites are in much closer proximity than in the northern US, yet racial prejudice is much more pronounced in the South.

Another example: in terms of social class, everyone experiences people from other social classes very day, but despite proximity the prejudices do not go away.

Then there's the odd fact that females and males have been living together for ... uh ... a very long time ... but ... well.

Clearly, proximity alone doesn't do the trick.

It's not about getting to know you. It's about how I go about getting to know you ...

Allport's Prejudice Scale traces how prejudice operates, from the low end of making jokes and assumptions about others, to the high end—or perhaps the lowest—of actual extermination of the other.

Allport contended that we have to go into an interaction with those unlike ourselves with an open mind

The Unitarian Universalist Association has an anti-prejudice program for congregations called Beyond Categorical Thinking. The term "categorical thinking" comes directly from the work of Allport, who in 1954 said, "The human mind must think with the aid of categories." Allport went on to say, "Once formed, categories are the basis for normal prejudgment. We cannot possibly avoid this process. Orderly living depends upon it."[1]

So, how do we go beyond categorical thinking? How do we get outside of our tribal thinking? Allport's "contact hypothesis" says that not only must we have contact with those not in our tribe, but the contact must be on equal terms and with common goals.

Equal terms. Common goals.

This explains why race relations don't improve much, despite proximity. It explains why maids and their employers don't see each other. Equal terms and common goals. It explains why females and males can have children together without ever really seeing each other.

Why are only 8 percent of US congregations integrated, despite years and years of trying?

We've been going about it all wrong. Congregations wait, in smug certitude that their preexisting terms and goals are—of course and obviously—the true and correct ones.

---

1. Allport, *Nature of Prejudice*, 41.

Equal terms. Common goals. These two things require respect across the divides, be they racial, economic, or religious.

Equal terms. Common goals. Were we to achieve these, those aliens might write in their star log a hundred thousand years hence, "Mistaken about *Homo sapiens*. Divisive tribalism vanished. Humanity flourishes."

Roadmaps for the Soul (or: Hunting, Gathering, Singing)

In "Tombstone Blues," a song released in 1965, Bob Dylan sang, "The National Bank at a profit sells roadmaps for the soul / To the old folks home and the college." In the context of the song, Bob clearly doesn't think this is a good thing. Commodifying the meaning of life?

Yes, well . . .

Suppose for a moment that all the religious and philosophical speculation through time, and all the art and architecture to boot, have been about the same thing as the hunting and the fishing, the gathering and farming. Suppose that all human actions—from the sacred to the profane—have been and are still . . . ways to survive. Ways for us to adapt to our environment and, perhaps, thrive.

Does such a supposition denigrate—or cheapen—all the blood and tears shed in service to the gods? Or in service to art? I don't think so.

Is a symphony less because it's an adaptive trait rather than a window onto absolute truth? What if the search for truth and meaning is itself an adaptive trait—a way of surviving?

Put this way, it's hard not to say, "Well, duh!" Yet we often don't go quite far enough. Yes, human activities of all sorts are attempts at survival. But if our search for truth and meaning in all its manifestations, from fine art to fine dining to religion, is an adaptive trait, doesn't it follow that the search for truth and meaning is an entirely human construct? It's filling a need but has no larger purpose.

Like most people, I searched for a "really true truth" for a long time. Hey, I'm a Baby Boomer; it's what we did. It was a brilliant marketing ploy. The tax dollars you lose giving churches tax-exempt status is $71 billion a year. That's a lot of moola for Moloch. (Full disclosure: as a minister, I ride that gravy train.)

The search for truth and meaning puts a lot of food on the table and a lot of money into retirement accounts for various sorts of people. No, this isn't about tax exemptions. It's about the price we are willing to pay purveyors of truth and meaning. After all, yoga alone is a $27-billion-a-year industry.

We pay a lot for truth and meaning, in bookstores, museums, churches, and storefront meditation centers. To repeat, I think that's great. It's an adaptive trait. Yet, it's good to remember that there is no one truth to find.

This particular survival trait only becomes problematic when we fall into the trap of thinking there's a truth out there to find. It's problematic when we begin paying a high price for one particular roadmap for the soul, or when those around us begin paying too high a price.

It's a great survival trait. Until someone gets hurt.

Yes, it's the search itself that is the answer. Not the answers.

Or the roadmaps.

A Semi-Private Idaho and Life in the Goldilocks Zone

> Living in your own private Idaho
> underground like a wild potato
> —The B52s

You've probably heard of the "Goldilocks Zone," that temperate place where H_2O exists in the form of water, that place where scientists speculate life might exist on other planets.

I think a Unitarian Universalist congregation should be a Goldilocks Zone where the free exchange of ideas concerning ultimate meaning and purpose flows like life-giving water. After all, the fourth principle of the Unitarian Universalist Association is "a free and responsible search for truth and meaning."

I know that actually the Unitarian Universalist Association principles are only agreements between congregations, underlining the right of each member congregation to respect the particular theological stance of the various congregations. But, in practice, these principles have been embraced more by individuals within congregations than between congregations, where there is pressure to conform to the franchise—a topic for another day.

I mention this because a congregation such as First Unitarian Society of Minneapolis has historically embraced humanism and has its own set of aspirations, the fourth of which is to "support one another's journey toward meaning and connection in the here and now."

That's a more humanist slant than the fourth principle of the UUA, but aimed toward the same ideal, a Goldilocks Zone for the free flow of ideas concerning ultimate meaning and purpose. This is the ideal. As with most ideals, our congregation falls short in reality. But we must continue to strive for the ideal. That's what ideals are for—to stretch us. Three methods help get us to the Goldilocks Zone:

1. Hit the pause button on being right.
2. Hang your inner judge and jury.
3. Trust everyone's path.

Easier said than done. But one way to get there is to become a pragmatist. As in the philosophy called pragmatism. Sure, you can remain an idealist or a cynic or whatever in other matters, but try pragmatism when it comes to creating a Goldilocks Zone in a congregational setting.

Listen to what psychologist and pragmatist philosopher William James had to say about that most contentious of issues, theism:

> If believing as though we have free will, or as if God exists, gets us the results we want, we will not only come to believe those things; they will be, pragmatically, true.

By "free will," James meant "non-theist," accruing to the theological understandings of the time. In that light, consider again what he said:

> If believing as though (there is no God), or as if God exists, gets us the results we want, we will not only come to believe those things; they will be, pragmatically, true.[1]

A pragmatist is a pragmatist due to a deep skepticism concerning the human ability to ascertain ultimate truth. Since pragmatists aren't confident that human beings can do that, pragmatists put air-quotes around "truth" and examine not what a truth is but how it affects human behavior.

In that light, notice what William James is saying: belief in a god or belief in no god works when it works. When it "gets us the results we want." Whichever way we choose, the path we are on becomes pragmatically "true."

If we can get there, we're in the Goldilocks Zone for multifaith communication and understanding.

This way of thinking led William James to write his great book *The Varieties of Religious Experience*, which makes most short lists for the greatest work of non-fiction from the twentieth century. And this way of thinking creates the Goldilocks Zone for the both "free" and "responsible" search that each of us must make for truth and meaning. Notice that this pragmatic approach accomplishes all three of my criteria for the Goldilocks Zone:

---

1. Cited in Watson, *Age of Atheists*.

1. Hit the pause button on being right.
2. Hang your inner judge and jury.
3. Trust everyone's path.

"But wait," perhaps you are saying, "my path is better!" Just add a couple of words to that statement: "My path is better *for me.*"

"But my beliefs are objectively true!" No: your beliefs are objectively true *for you.* Both pragmatically and scientifically, objective reality is always subject to further examination. The pragmatists knew this in their bones. "Truth" for them is only a tool.

Consider the words of a couple more great pragmatists. Philosopher George Santayana said, "There is no cure for birth and death save to enjoy the interval by discerning and manifesting the good without attempting to retain it."

Let it go, Santayana is saying.

Consider the words of pragmatic philosopher John Dewey: "Growth itself is the only moral end."

Who am I—and who are you—Dewey points out, to judge the religious and philosophical understandings of another person? Maybe you have a PhD in religious studies. That's great. Maybe you were born UU and have a very open mind and no emotional baggage about religion. Bully for you. Remind yourself: anyone who walks into a Unitarian Universalist congregation for the first time is saying, "I need to think about this ultimate-meaning-and-purpose stuff. I'm not satisfied with the off-the-rack, one-size-fits-all answers."

Remember that none of us has the ultimate answers—the answers that work for everybody. I don't have all the answers. I'm still thinking. And I get paid to think about these things. I thought about titling this section, "What I Really, Really Think about God (This Week)."

Try this: avoid going "underground like a wild potato." Share your subjectivity but remember that it is subjectivity, and each of us lives in some sort of private Idaho. Insisting on our own rightness leads to an icy world; saying there's only one way leads to a steamed world.

The Goldilocks Zone, where the fresh water flows, is only possible when we get outside our own stuff and listen.

Let's Agree to Agree on Subjectivity

Pragmatism. Pragmatists say, if it works for you, it's true. I know some find that a bit hard to swallow. Idealists, for instance. So, allow me to try to get to the same spot from a different direction.

For an idealist, there's something out there that's true. Idealists will admit that we see the world as we have learned to see the world; that our seeing affects us and those around us. It affects the world. Our seeing does not, however, make the world into what we see. The world is always as it is.

For example, I may decide that the tree in front of my house is possessed by an evil spirit. I may perform various rites to exorcise the evil spirit. I may even cut the tree down and burn it, thinking that extremity will at last do away with the demon.

Perhaps I even believe that I have succeeded in exorcising the demon and feel better about it all. Whatever I think, the fact of the matter is a dead tree, not an exorcised demon. One is measurable; the other is not.

Before going looking for something, it's good to know what you're looking for. What do we want in a god? I suspect the answer is: meaning and purpose in human life, a moral direction to the universe where the good and bad get what they deserve, perhaps even a cheerful afterlife where everyone is twenty-five years old and we get to talk with our grandmothers . . . and hang out with Abraham Lincoln.

That sort of thing.

This is the sort of god that the mainline monotheisms at one time posited for us. It's the sort of afterlife promised by the sort of churches I attended as a child. Then I read Sigmund Freud (as did the generation a century before me). And I began to think there is a big problem with this god concept: it sounds suspiciously like wish fulfillment. And it can't be measured.

Mainline Christian theologians don't paint this picture of God anymore. They have gone in two broad directions: process theology ("god" is in the processes of nature), or the psychological route, saying: Okay, we've got two things here: there is that which is inside the human brain, and that which is outside the human brain.

This is, after all, how we experience reality: the personal and the impersonal. "God" is subjective—inside the human brain. God is not in the scientifically measurable outside realm.

These theologians will argue that putting god in the category of human subjectivity is not a denigration or demotion of god. Lots of important things exist only in our subjectivity. For example, I have spent much of my life fighting for "justice." (Again with the quotes!)

"Justice" is a human subjectivity. "Justice" does not exist in the outside world as a measurable thing. You can't weigh it. Consider: "justice" has no meaning to a crocodile. A crocodile cannot act justly, at least from a human perspective.

Is justice an insignificant or untrue concept because it is the product of the human mind? Admittedly, we can say, "That was a just court decision" or "That was an unjust court decision." But those are instances in time. They are not the concept "justice."

Groups of human beings agree on the subjectivity called "justice."

And the same is true of the several concepts of God. God is a shared consensual subjectivity among various groups. A shared consensual subjectivity. We agree that our subjectivities agree with each other and that the concept "God" is this way or that way . . . for us. That's why various faith traditions require creeds said aloud: they are attempting to keep the shared consensual subjectivity similar in various minds.

Now clearly this concept of God pushes the idea of human understanding beyond the true/false dichotomy. Beyond the dichotomy that objective is true and subjective is false or at least suspicious. But consider: so far as we know, human consciousness is the most complex thing in the universe. So let's give ourselves a little credit—maybe everything isn't a zero or a one.

Computers are better than we are at chess. But not at writing poems. Or symphonies.

Everything is not zero or one. Crocodiles or rocks don't write poetry; people write poetry. And "God" is poetry. God is a human art. Knowledge is more than information.

It may well be that "religion" or "god" or "gods" exist in the same category as we consider abstract concepts such as "justice"—in objective reality these concepts don't exist, yet the human brain is capable of creating these concepts out of the chaotic particulars of human experience.

Fact is, no matter how many times the US Supreme Court makes a really, really stupid decision, I'm going to keep working for what I see as justice. For many people, the same is true for "God"—despite all the evidence to the contrary, it is a concept that still makes sense to them.

This is why, despite the fact that I don't share the subjectivity called God, I don't get angry and shout about it. It can even be fun—and instructive—to talk over our subjectivities. We might even learn something from each other.

Wounds and Healers

I sat for two weeks by the bedside of my dying father. There's nothing like days and days of sitting with a dying person for focusing on what is important and what is not. In the end, we turn into pulse, breathing, a few bodily functions. And then—slowly in the case of a hospice patient—those cease.

And I am like just about everyone who goes through such an ordeal: I ask a simple question: "What is the meaning of the suffering?"

As a young writer, I read everything I could find on the subject of writing. One of the books that impressed me at the time was written by novelist John Gardner, a book called *Moral Fiction*. If my memory serves me, it is in that book that Gardner argues that every writer has a wound that drives his or her writing. By "wound" Gardner meant a psychological trauma so devastating that writers revisit and seek to rewrite this trauma constantly in their minds. (This theory predates the concept of Post-Traumatic Stress Disorder, PTSD.)

It's not surprising that Gardner should have developed such a theory, since he had suffered a severe trauma in his own life. John Gardner grew up on a farm and, as is often the case, he drove tractors when he was quite young. One day Gardner was driving a tractor and his brother was riding on the back. His brother fell off and was killed by the implement the tractor was pulling.

For the rest of his life, Gardner replayed and replayed in his mind the image of his brother falling. He blamed himself for his brother's death. He never stopped asking himself, "What could I have done?" (Gardner himself eventually died in a motorcycle accident.)

As I made my own attempts at writing, I discovered that the old cliché "truth is stranger than fiction" is partially true because writers can't help attempting to make sense of the random happenings of the world. The human mind can't help trying.

Creative writing is, if nothing else, an assertion of the self in the face of what often appears to be a completely random reality. It's the human need to create meaning that makes fiction less strange than truth.

But it is not true that only writers have wounds. Sure, some people become writers because of the need to process trauma. But the fact is, as the Buddha observed long ago, life itself is loss. We suffer because nothing is permanent except change.

(I know, I know—I've met the random individual who claims to have had a charmed, Pollyanna life. Of course I'm too polite to say the obvious: "Just wait.")

Think for a moment about something you are hanging on to that isn't good for you . . . something that you just can't let go of. Something that makes you cringe when you think of it. Something that you replay over and over, like an old movie, in your head.

Allow me to ask a very simple question: What do you gain by hanging on to what you are hanging on to? Is it that your wounds have become old friends? Whatever would you do without them? Perhaps they give you meaning: "Hey, I'm not nobody, I'm a victim!" As Shakespeare put it,

> I will be flesh and blood,
> For there was never yet philosopher
> That could endure the toothache patiently,
> However they have writ the style of gods
> And made a push at chance and sufferance.[1]

I think that Shakespeare is driving at the insight psychologist Carl Jung had when he coined the phrase "wounded healer." It isn't that therapists or ministers or anybody else have the answers to life's wounds. It is, rather, that dwelling on those wounds drives many of us to be therapists or ministers or philosophers.

Pain—both physical and psychological—makes us individualists. We do well to get over that selfishness, however, and reach out because the cure for pain lies in that reaching out. However we write the style of our gods, as Shakespeare put it, we must accept our flesh and blood and dependency on others before healing begins. As philosopher Crispin Sartwell puts it, "When you consult your experience, the fact that you are a body is more obvious than that two plus two equals four."

This is perhaps not an entirely reassuring insight. We would rather see our healers as experts and ourselves in charge. But that attitude, too, is a fall into individualism. The answer is in reaching out. The Chinese Chan Buddhist Hsu Yun said it simply:

---

1. *Much Ado About Nothing*, act 5, scene 1.

Here is the beautiful truth—
saints and sinners are the same
from the start.

Buddhist wisdom says there are three ways we naturally approach anything: desire, aversion, or indifference. For the sake of convenience, I call them, "yum," "eeeeewwww," and "zzzzzz."

I see a slice of cheesecake. "Yum!" I love cheesecake. I desire the slice of cheesecake. I grab it . . . five hundred calories down my gullet.

I see a squirrel that's been hit by a car. "Eeeewwww!" Aversion. I look away.

Then there's indifference: trees along the route to work, for example. Those tchotchkes around the house that you haven't dusted in months. Indifference. You just don't see them. "Zzzzzz."

I swallow the cheesecake before I even have time to enjoy it. I'm too caught up in my aversion at the sight of the wounded squirrel to help. I don't bother looking up to see the gift that simple things like sycamore trees or a souvenir from long ago can bring.

Desire. Aversion. Indifference. These are the reactions we naturally have when our brains are on autopilot. And Buddhists say these lead to our suffering. We go through our thoughtless lives wanting, rejecting, and ignoring. And it's always about me, me, and me.

How can we get out of that cycle?

Buddhism teaches that we have to find a place of equanimity—calmness, composure, evenness of temper.

But how can I keep evenness of temper when there's cheesecake around? How can I stay composed when I experience disgusting or frightening things? How can I be composed when I'm staring absently out the window and don't even see what's in front of my nose?

Equanimity is about being mindful—aware—no matter how tempting, disgusting, or boring something is. Equanimity is about living in the here and now fully. Fully in touch with what surrounds us, without saying "yum," "eeeeewwww," or "zzzzzz."

Equanimity is clearly a way of bringing our aspirations into our actions, of bringing what we wish we did and what we do into closer relationship.

Easier said than done! But that's how it is with ethical thinking: it is always about either paddling upstream—against the currents of human nature—or making attempts to explain why. It's about how human nature is OK after all, at least in certain circumstances. Things like war, murder, torture, xenophobia, oppression. That sort of thing.

Sigmund Freud—no fan of religion—argued that culture does much the same thing as religion. It functions to mitigate the fearsomeness of nature, to reconcile us to the randomness and cruelty of fate, and to explain why culture itself makes so many problems for us.

It seems to me that both culture and religion (perhaps because the separation of church and state is a modern invention) are pretty good at creating duty, because both contain carrots and sticks. They create duty but not necessarily (or commonly) responsibility, which is a personal choice unaffected by carrots or sticks. Antoine de Saint-Exupéry put it this way: "Civilization rests upon what it exacts from its people, not from what it furnishes them." The same can perhaps be said of most of religion.

Responsibility is a personal choice. A choice arrived at (or not) by each of us. How we get there depends upon the lives and circumstances we experience. Responsibility is a personal ideal. We live up to it.

Which brings me back to equanimity. It, too, is an ideal—we're always going to default to "yum" or "eeeeewwww" or "zzzzzz."

Equanimity. The Buddhists think it's a good way to act. It's what made the Stoics stoic.

Equanimity. It's a choice.

It's a truism in looking at prospective seminary students to wonder if they are recent converts to Twelve Step programs. Or newly divorced. Or have recently encountered some other trauma. Are these people signing on to be Karl Jung's "wounded healers"? I'm certainly not saying that's a bad thing. It's a natural human thing: "Here is my wound. Here is my suffering. Where is the meaning?" Then: "How can I help others who have been through what I've been through and worse?"

And here's the biggest paradox of it all: just as meaning and responsibility are choices arrived at from individual lives, they are about sharing. Sharing with other human beings. After all, my "yum" or "eeeeewwww" or "zzzzzz" may be someone else's master's thesis or research project.

Isn't it amazing that—no matter what may happen to us—we can be confident that there are people who will take care of us? This is confidence in the human spirit, the confidence of humanism. It is a religion (if you will) not of victimhood and suffering but of creativity and compassion.

Tinfoil Hats and the Examined Life

Let's say I tell you that from now on I'm wearing a tinfoil hat. What does that say to you? Crazy? Paranoid? Safe from the mental meddling of governments and/or extraterrestrials?

It's shorthand, isn't it? A tinfoil hat says crazy or paranoid, or safe, not because of anything inherent in the tinfoil hat, but because we equate wearing a tinfoil hat with a set of behaviors that could be well described as crazy or paranoid or staying safe—"tinfoil hat" is a symbol for a set of beliefs—that, for example, space aliens or perhaps one government or another is sending messages into my brain by electric means.

The first known appearance of a tinfoil hat is in a science fiction story published in 1927 by the evolutionary biologist Julian Huxley. In that story, tinfoil hats prevent interference from mental telepathy.

If you look for how tinfoil hats work on Yahoo Answers, you will discover this advice:

> Tin foil does not work. I tried aluminum foil for my first thought screen helmet in 1998 and it was a failure. Thought screens made from velostat work. I've been making them since 1999 and sending them to abductees all over the world for free for 13 years.

In case you're like me and didn't know, Velostat is a packing material used to block electronic effects. So it goes.

I want to notice two things about this brief look at tinfoil hats. First, "tinfoil hat" has come to mean something way beyond merely a hat made of a particular material. And, second, how quickly we rocket from a discussion of tinfoil hats to a discussion of more efficient hats to evade thought surveillance.

Both of these things have to do with the human imagination. How the human imagination works. We make symbols. Then, often, we fall into the trap of treating a symbol as if it were a reality. We easily mistake symbols, and symbolic statements, for literal truths.

The simplest example is perhaps flags. We create a flag to symbolize a nation or some other grouping of people. Then we create rules and customs around how flags must be treated.

I've heard people debate whether a particular piece of cloth is a flag or only bunting—because you can burn bunting, but burning a flag might get you into trouble.

We create a symbol, then we treat the symbol as a reality. The flag becomes the nation. And so on.

Educator Hugh Mearns had something to say about this propensity back in 1899 when he wrote a poem in response to a brouhaha in the town of Antigonish, Nova Scotia concerning a ghost sighting. One of the poem's verses goes like this:

> Last night I saw upon the stair,
> A little man who wasn't there,
> He wasn't there again today
> Oh, how I wish he'd go away . . .

It appears that we can make symbols of things that aren't there at all. And then the symbol becomes a thing we can imagine.

We enter into pretend realms very early in childhood—you be Batman; I'll be Joker. I'm an elephant. I'm a unicorn. When we play these games, we agree to certain rules. We agree to be bound by the logic of the game. Just as do the folks who wear tinfoil hats or who set out to make a better tinfoil hat. Or who imagine little men on stairs that aren't there.

We can go to a murder mystery dinner party set in the 1920s and act as if we have murdered someone. Or act as if we are a Belgian detective. We can go to a Renaissance festival where corporate lawyers become barmaids and carpenters become knights.

We choose a game, we agree to obey the rules of the game, and then we act . . . as if.

This is how fiction works. There are all sorts of fictions, each written according to the rules of the game that the author asks us to play. Perhaps the novel is naturalistic; in that case, everything that happens will happen according to the observable and describable rules of the universe.

We can have "magical realism," in which the world operates more or less as it does in our own world, but occasionally odd things happen—such as people flying away.

We can also have fantasy—that is, a world in which the rules we know do not apply. But even there, notice, there *are* rules of the game. Devotees of Star Trek or of World of Warcraft will be quick to point out when an action goes outside the rules of that particular fantasy world.

We agree to the rules of a particular form of government. Or of economics. Of of religion. In these cases, usually, we have very little in the way of choice about playing the game; we are born in places where a set of games with rules are already in place—this is called culture and tradition.

Those who choose to ignore the rules are ostracized or punished. The rules of the games called culture and tradition often insist that you *will* see the little man on the stair—or at least say you do—even if you cannot see the little man.

•

However, the difference between knowing you are playing a game with rules and thinking you are seeing reality are very different things, aren't they?

Some games we choose, and some we don't. No one is born wearing a tinfoil hat. Or saluting a particular flag. Or worshiping a particular god. Mostly, such games with their particular rules are forced upon us by geography or social status or educational attainment or mental health.

"Is he really equating tinfoil hats and patriotism?" you might be asking. Yes, I am. Because I think the examined life requires that sort of examination. Until we see the games we are enmeshed in with some clarity, we have seen neither truth nor reality. We have not examined life.

What's your game? Do tinfoil hats come in handy?

Humanism and Theology

The most common definition of the word "theology" is "the study of the nature of god and religious belief." The "theo" and "logy" that go to make up the word means "god-words" or "god-logic."

Thus, strictly speaking, many humanists don't have much to say about theology, since we don't believe in the god-concept anyway.

In this way, "theology" is much like the word "atheist." Many object to "a-theist" because we don't want to be defined for not being something we don't think matters much anyway. It's an old-fashioned concept, this "theist." Many prefer to be called "post-theist," if we have to be called anything at all from that perspective.

This is a loooooong way of going about saying that we are often stuck with the word "theology" when what we are talking about is the clarification of morals, ethics, meaning, and values. Theists must come up with what they think the nature of God is, then decide upon what their ethics, morals, and values are based on that God-concept (or they have all of that imposed upon them by a specific religious tradition.)

Humanists don't do that. Humanists believe that human beings have evolved with morals, ethics, and values, and that we have the capacity to hone and modify those based on what we see in the here and now.

Humanists can do "theo-logy" too. It's just that we don't need the god-words. We have our own! Perhaps that was best summed up in 1837 when Charles Darwin, the year after returning from his fateful journey on HMS Beagle, wrote:

> If we choose to let conjecture run wild, then animals, our fellow brethren in pain, diseases, death, suffering and famine—our slaves in the most laborious works, our companions in our amusements—they may partake our origin in one common ancestor—we may be all netted together.

Humanists "choose to let conjecture run wild." Science has shown, and we know, that "we are all netted together" in the "interdependent web of all existence."

We are obligated to act on this knowledge.

The same is true with the word "sacred." Sounds nice to some people. The word means "connected with God (or gods) or consecrated to God (or gods)." Since many humanists don't believe any gods exist, it is a bit difficult to be connected or consecrated to one. I suppose the best translation for the word is "really, really important." Or, perhaps we should stick with the "connected" in the definition and say that "sacred" translates as "deeply connected with all of life and all of the cosmos."

Reason Is Dead; Long Live . . . Advanced Hindsight

Justice. It may be a meal best served cold, but not on an empty stomach. Israeli Neuroscientist and business professor Shai Danziger studied the correlation between food and the likelihood that a judge will grant prisoners parole.

In the morning, just after breakfast, the chances of parole are high—around 65 percent. But this number quickly plummets until . . . the judge takes a snack break. After the snack, there's a spike of leniency, then down again until lunch.

Professor Danziger points out that making decisions is tough on our brains. Soon, we suffer from "choice overload," and we begin to take the easy choice as our blood sugar drops.

Good sleep, rest, and good food are the stuff of good decisions, even the stuff of justice.

Justice. Rationality.

The Western world has long viewed the human mind through a metaphor Plato used: a charioteer driving two horses—one horse reason, the other horse passion; one noble, the other not. This dualism, this idea that our reason struggles to keep irrational passion in check, is the basis of Western philosophy, the basis of Western religion. We have come to understand thought and action as a dichotomy of mind and body, of head and heart.

There's one problem with this way of understanding: it isn't true. There is no body/mind split. There is no head/heart split. It's all flesh and chemicals. Our minds are not a charioteer driving two unruly horses. It's more like we're riding one horse, but we aren't holding the reins. When we arrive at the place the horse chooses to go, we create reasons for why that's exactly where we wanted to be.

Justice is dependent on blood sugar? More than we'd like to think. What has revealed this fact to us? Reason.

How very odd!

The more we learn about ourselves, the more we know that we are not rational creatures most of the time. In the case of most decisions, we have already made up our minds before we realize it, and our rationality merely acts as a village explainer, justifying our actions to ourselves and sometimes others. Just as in the free-ranging horse metaphor.

Yet, paradoxically, the human enterprise has been best served by reason—in the scientific method, in mathematics, in scholarship. What has been called "the Enlightenment project" depended upon these conscious acts.

What is and is not threatened by our contemporary understanding of reason? The justice system, for one thing. That appears to be less just than we might have hoped.

Democracy? Attack ads have done what the armies of tyrants could not.

Capitalism? Free market capitalism depends upon a rational market. The field of behavioral economics has shown this to be as much a myth as Plato's charioteer.

Reason isn't what it used to be. Dan Ariely, a Duke professor of psychology and behavioral economics, has opened a study center at the university he calls the Center for Advanced Hindsight. Dr. Ariely's research joins the work of scores of neuroscientists demonstrating that the Western Enlightenment, with it's Reason with a capital R and the projects that flow from it, from jurisprudence to democracy to capitalism, all have feet of clay. Swift-boating, not cold logic, will drive the actions of both nations and shoppers.

Our new understanding also shows that when it comes to what is real and true, the dead reckoning of reason may be anemic and difficult, but it's all we have. Descartes, Spinoza, and the rest knew this, as they looked out on the demon-haunted worlds they were born into. We forget at our peril.

Soapy Cilantro and Tasty Gods

Cilantro. It's a polarizing vegetable. Many love it. Many hate it. For some, it is just the fresh touch needed to make Mexican and Thai cuisine perfect. For others, cilantro tastes like Ivory soap.

An unbridgeable chasm, it would appear.

Three genes have been identified as having to do with cilantro perception. It's nature—three whole genes. A little investigation, however, offers hope. Though the hatred of cilantro is due to our genes, nurture may come to the rescue.

It is possible—at least for some people—to reverse cilantro aversion by making and consuming it in a pesto. (Chopping changes the chemical makeup.)

In this, cilantro is much like God, isn't it? Each of us believes or doesn't. We know some of our beliefs are due to nurture. How many are due to nature?

Take as an example something you've probably noticed: "aha!" moments of conversion from one side to the other—theist to a-theist—don't appear to happen all that often. Some are born loving cilantro. Some are born hating it. Few bother to make pesto and change cilantro categories.

Again, how much of theism is nature?

Studies show that the number of people claiming to believe in divinity is dropping steadily. But how much of that drop is due to "aha!" conversions and how much is due to the mainstreaming of atheism as atheists and agnostics come out of the closet?

For example, sadly, we will never know how many people did and did not believe in god in the grand old days of Christendom in Europe. The choice was . . . be Christian or be dead.

We do know that most of the European population had no choice about converting to Christianity. The local dukes, earls, and other strongpersons said . . . be Christian or be dead. Some chose death. Most, I suspect, chose silence.

There is one glaring counterexample. The savagery of the Vikings was long "proven" by using the example of their attack on the English monastery of Lindisfarne. Killing unarmed monks is, without question, a savage thing to do.

Now we know, however, that the attackers were retaliating against Christians because of the brutal policies of the emperor Charlemagne, who pronounced a death sentence on any "pagan" unwilling to convert. The Vikings at Lindisfarne had lost loved ones to those monks they chose to kill.

God is also like cilantro in the nature of arguments for and against god: there's no logical argument for the concept of god.

There are some things that appear to be the case because they appear to be the case. For example, it appears that convincing people that free will does or does not exist is a pointless task. After all, anyone who believes in free will can't be convinced that free will is a fiction. And, were he or she to "convert" to the opposite view, we could say . . . it was because of free will. Or not.

You see the problem.

The concept of free will is not like cilantro.

Another example: it appears that humanity will never learn to time travel. It appears that's the case because . . . no one is showing up from the future. Sure, there are dodges—that we will in the future also learn to be invisible, for example, or learn how to be in another dimension and therefore undetectable. Still, barring some major changes in how people do things, it appears time travel will never become possible.

Whether or not time travel will occur is not like cilantro.

But belief in a god or gods: it's a feeling, a taste.

It's yummy or soapy.

So . . . perhaps, like cilantro, the choice to believe or not is best left up to the individual. For some, it's yummy. For some, soapy. Nature, nurture.

But fussing over it? Fuhgettaboudit.

(Note: I've just written something that would get me arrested and/or killed in most times and places. Thanks, Constitution. No thanks, RFRA.)

Subjectivity, Existence, and the Stories We Tell Ourselves

All of us are born into a world we do not understand. Every human being ever born has found the same. What has humanity done with the mystery of our existence? We tell stories.

And thus, slowly, we learn. We learn stories. Stories that explain the origin of the universe. Stories that explain the origin of the things on this planet. Stories that tell us how to act in this mysterious, beautiful, and tragic world.

Some stories are as old as humanity. Some stories are as new as the latest science. Some stories have agendas.

All are stories.

We experience worlds within worlds. We experience both the natural and the social worlds of which we are a part. We understand little of either of them intuitively. Mostly, our understandings are cultural, based on the stories we learn.

One of the first people to tell me how the world worked was my grandmother, who was illiterate and had spent her life as a sharecropper's wife, giving birth to eleven children. It's not, in other words, that she did not know "reality," but her reality was . . . of a type.

She consulted her imagination more often than she consulted observable facts.

Her god was one that kept constant watch and kept a tally of every sin and every good deed. This god handed out favors and rewards and punishments. This god was like a European king.

Despite the magic and even whimsy of my grandmother's world, I found her world frightening.

It's good, I think, to reflect sometimes on those people who were formative in our thinking. The people who told us stories. And why we continue to carry those stories with us. The ones that we still believe. The ones that we don't believe any longer.

One of the things that I've learned since I left my grandmother's world is that there are at least two ways for things to "exist." One is existence without need of experience. Oxygen is like that. Canyons and mountains are like that. They are there.

The second way to exist is an existence only in experience—fear or happiness, for example. We don't doubt that these exist, but they exist only in an individual consciousness. It isn't that happiness does not exist—it's just that happiness only exists as a result of being.

These distinctions get difficult. Energy and matter exist in the first sense—they are just there. Space and time exist in the second sense—they are relative to consciousness. Yet, space and time appear to exist more like mountains than they do like fear or joy.

Now: my grandmother, and fundamentalists like her of whatever stripe, will argue that their god exists or does not exist exactly as does oxygen and canyons—that gods are there whether we are experiencing them or not. (In this scenario, an atheist is merely someone who say, "No, they don't exist.")

What fundamentalists—or perhaps we should call them merely literalists . . . What literalists—be they Christian, Muslim, or atheist—miss is the other way of being: that which exists only in experience. This feeling is no more valid or invalid than saying something is too salty or not spicy enough. In this sense, gods exist because someone experiences a god or gods—feels them.

But many gods are not completely subjective, because groups choose to agree on certain properties for their subjectivities, which we can call culturally conditioned experience. Groups agree to agree on some particular gods with particular attributes as a group. Thus, many god-concepts are a shared subjectivity. They are the stories of the culture.

My grandmother had agreed to experience a god that was much like a European king. This was the god agreed upon by the Europeans who had settled in the Ohio River Valley where she and I were born. My grandmother didn't know that she had agreed to that subjectivity, but she had. As did most of my family. This story was their story. I have chosen not to agree with that concept. I have a different story.

One way to get our minds around this is to think about a holiday—Thanksgiving, perhaps. Thanksgiving exists because whole groups agree that there is such a thing as the US Thanksgiving and that certain things occur on or around that day.

Thanksgiving exists as a shared subjectivity—we all make it happen. It is a story we tell. If we all stopped believing in Thanksgiving, it would cease to exist.

So much of our reality is the stories we tell ourselves. Wisdom lies in knowing which stores we are telling ourselves and why. Wisdom lies in knowing when to consult our imaginations and when to consult the facts on the ground.

Where Is the I in Me?

A child falls and begins screaming. It's common. You did it as a child. I did it. What happens next?

For me, my parents said, "Get up off the floor! Boys don't cry!"

If a kid falls and starts screaming at an upscale preschool nearby, I'm more likely to hear, "You feel sad!" Or, "That's frustrating, isn't it?" Or, "You're so angry!"

What's the difference between the two parental responses? Fact is, any time I cried as a child, I got the same response: "Boys don't cry." Consequently, I learned to suppress my emotions rather than expressing them.

That child outside the upscale preschool, on the other hand, is being taught the difference between anger and sadness and frustration and fear and embarrassment. That child is developing a palate of emotions with nuance. That child is developing "emotional intelligence."

Kids treated as I was learn that emotions need to be suppressed. We learn "men don't do that." We learn "women are hysterical." And so the clichés go, 'round and around. And so does the drinking and drugs and physical violence and abuse that come as a consequence of the suppression of emotion.

Allow me to add that my parents were preparing me for the world that they lived in: working-class people do well to learn to be very careful about emotion. It is potentially dangerous to let the boss see your emotion. My father was in the Boilermakers Union. You don't cry among your fellow Boilermakers. And you don't get angry when the boss yells at you.

We were also farmers, and farmers in traditional communities aren't traditionally allowed to get angry either. You can't show anger when the bank won't give you a loan . . . and on and on. It's a life of oppression and suppression in which a show of emotion can be interpreted as dangerous. That's the world I was prepared for.

We call the result "stable." But at what cost to both the individual and society?

Professor Ronald F. Levant and colleagues did a study called "A Multicultural Investigation of Masculinity Ideology and Alexithymia." It wasn't a bestseller, but the study tells us what we already have intuited: in many social groups, men are afraid to express emotion, especially in the presence of other men.

"Alexithymia" describes the result of this suppression: an inability to describe emotions, an inability to sustain social connections, and an inability to sustain interpersonal relationships.

The result is a socially created sociopath. The result is a dangerous person created by the desire to live up to the social definition of masculinity. That pretty well describes the men in my extended family. Think for a moment about how many—and different—lives you lead. Partner. Friend. Manager. Coworker. Tinkerer, tailor, soldier, spy . . .

We learn to use different vocabularies in these different niches. We learn to express our emotions differently. In addition, as the dad of two children in the GLBTQ alphabet soup, I know that the gender binary is an inconvenient fiction. Men aren't from Mars and women from Venus. We come from many planets, or, as comedian George Carlin pointed out, "Men are from Earth; women are from Earth. Deal with it." Still, we have an obligation to try to use our words, no matter what planet we're from.

The twentieth-century writer Anais Nin started writing when she was eleven. She continued, obsessively writing of her inner life, for more than sixty years. She said this:

> I am a series of moods and sensations. I play a thousand roles. I weep when I find others play them for me. My real self is unknown . . . I create a myth and a legend, a lie, a fairy tale, a magical world, and one that collapses every day . . .[1]

It isn't that Nin had some super-complex emotional life. Or that she was mentally ill. Rather, she had the tenacity to pursue her many selves to the essence of the self. Much like the Buddha. And, like the Buddha, she discovered there isn't one. There is no constant self. The evidence is right before our eyes. And right behind them too. What we have instead is an ocean of sensation and reaction. We have emotions—some fleeting, some stable enough to be called moods. These add up to what we call a self. Yet it's a fiction.

---

1. Nin, *Diary of Anais Nin*, vol. 4.

The dangerous and damaging idea behind this insistence on a stable self is what has been called "soul" in the Western tradition. That tradition tells us that the soul is incarnated—lives in the flesh for a time. Then goes somewhere forever, still constituted as the self that lived on Earth. In some traditions the soul is rewarded with heaven or hell. In others the soul blissfully resides . . . well, somewhere.

Such an idea is a dangerous illusion. The only constant is change. And the self and the soul it creates are stories we tell ourselves. The mad urge to maintain a constant self creates madness.

When we figure that out, the Buddha said, we are enlightened. Anais Nin put it this way: "I see myself and my life each day differently. What can I say? The facts lie."

B-liefs, A-liefs, and Seeing the Way Things Are

Tis education forms the common mind,

Just as the twig is bent, the tree's inclined.

—ALEXANDER POPE

ONE OF THE MAJOR tourist attractions in Chicago is the Willis Tower, formerly the Sears Tower and also formerly the tallest building in the world. Upon reaching the 103rd floor, visitors have the opportunity to walk out on "The Ledge," glass boxes that reach four feet past the outer walls of the building.

More interesting than the magnificent view is the reactions of visitors. Walking out onto clear glass 103 stories up is scary. And fun. And exhilarating. And some simply can't bring themselves to do it.

An ad for the building says, "Get out on the ledge if you dare!"

The glass floor consists of three layers of half-inch-thick glass and is designed to hold five tons. You're not going to fall through the floor. So. What scares people?

Tamar Gendler, Professor of Philosophy and Cognitive Science at Yale, has named what is happening an "alief." An alief is something that hits you out of the blue. Out of the recesses of your psyche. You "a-lieve" from the gut. Your a-lief says, "Freeze! You're going to fall."

You "be-lieve" just the opposite. Your mind, your reason, tells you that The Ledge is well engineered and is there merely as a thrilling curiosity.

•

I find the believe/alieve distinction valuable (in a be-lieve sort of way). Feeling you are going to fall through the glass floor is gut, immediate. You can reason yourself out of it. You may even bring your frozen legs to carry you out onto the glass. You may even laugh at yourself for being afraid. But if human beings didn't have the alief reaction, The Ledge would be a waste of money, not a major tourist draw.

Poet Alexander Pope formulated the point: "Just as the twig is bent, the tree's inclined."

I belong to a clergy group made up of Muslims, Jews, Christians, and humanist me. We do public debates, trying to model ways that religious dialogue can be done without resort to anger and name-calling. After expressing my agnosticism, I'm often asked something along the lines of, "If you were bleeding and dying by the side of the road, wouldn't you pray?"

I answer as honestly as I can. Yes, I would pray. Not because doing so proves the existence of supernatural forces, but because I grew up in a religious tradition that taught intercessory prayer. I don't believe it, but I will always a-lieve it.

This twig was bent by fundamentalism.

And, by the way, I'm not going out onto that glass floor, either.

White Privilege: "Kumbaya" Won't Cut It

A sad fact: many things that are good for society or the Earth itself are not good for me, me, me. Higher taxes hurt people like me. A livable minimum wage costs people like me. Fair trade costs me money. Carbon cap-and-trade hurts the pocketbooks of people like me, me, me.

A sad fact: wealth can be fairly distributed in three ways: philanthropy, taxes, revolution.

I can live in delusion and sing "Kumbaya" and say I'm in solidarity with all those other people—then do nothing—or I can get out there and break down White Privilege. And American Privilege. And Human Privilege, come to that. I can't get there through studying the problem, or guilt, or by singing "Kumbaya."

Edward Bernays was the "father of mass marketing." His most influential book, called *Propaganda* and published in 1928, is the bestselling book on political psychology of all time. (It has recently become a favorite among business people in China.)

Parenthetically, when Bernays saw that the word "propaganda" had negative connotations, he invented the term "public relations." Bernays believed that a democratic society required what he called "hidden governors."

Bernays is probably most famous for breaking the taboo against women smoking in public. He was hired by a tobacco company to convince women to smoke. He hired a group of models who marched in a parade in New York City. On cue, and in front of the cameras, the models lit up their cigarettes, called in the press release "Torches of Freedom." And soon every trendy flapper was smoking.

Bernays feared what he termed "herd mentality." He thought that the bourgeoisie—the upper-middle class—had deposed the kings, but had, by the 1920s, been in turn deposed by the working-class masses. He was convinced that the way for the upper-middle class to re-establish power was through propaganda. Uh, I mean public relations . . .

A study of his career is a study in bad ideas becoming popular. And I think we have to admit that his experiment worked. The privileged are still in power, perhaps more securely now than ever. And the poor watch the endless parade of bait and switch.

The concept of privilege does not imply that someone did not work hard for her or his stuff. Or work hard for his or her accomplishments. It means that the stuff and accomplishments she and he get a chance to work for are largely based on arbitrary factors such as geography, time, gender, and the religious and racial attitudes of the place and time of his and her birth.

In the United States, privilege boils down to exactly what Bernays and the people who hired him were: European, male, heterosexual, well educated. I can join a good liberal church and sing "Kumbaya" and let those market forces continue to work for me me, me, me. Or . . .

It's a burden. Those who do not believe in supernatural forces easily see how arbitrary privilege is: we did nothing to deserve it. It is not the choice of, or a reward from, supernatural forces. The very arbitrariness of privilege tells us that privilege is unjust. Furthermore, the realization of this arbitrariness tells us that we have an obligation to undo the effects of privilege, even though we may be directly benefiting from said privilege.

I don't doubt that those Chinese business folks currently studying the methods Bernays touted will develop their very own special form of privilege.

North Americans of European descent are born with privileges based on circumstances few of us had anything to do with—the genocide of the peoples who owned the land where we are; the unpaid labor of African slaves for hundreds of years; the exploitation of various immigrant groups; the exploitation of the working class for hundreds of years; the exploitation of poorer and smaller nations; biased tax structures . . . et cetera, et cetera, et cetera.

But these actions are not in the past—because the wealth and power accumulated through these actions are not in the past. The solution is not as simple as passing laws against racial profiling; the solution isn't as simple as changing the hearts and minds of those who benefit so that we feel sad all the way to the bank.

The solution is the redistribution of the wealth and power accumulated by the actions. And, yes, that would look exactly like the sort of democracy that Edward Bernays feared. And, yes, that would make many privileged White people sad.

Beyond Mansplaining

Mansplaining—the song "You are Sixteen Going on Seventeen" by Rogers and Hammerstein perhaps epitomizes it:

> Totally unprepared are you
> To face a world of men
> Timid and shy and scared are you
> Of things beyond your ken

The composition date of that is 1959. Betty Friedan's book *The Feminine Mystique* didn't appear until 1963, and it's obvious why such a book had to be written. Friedan's book is credited with starting what's come to be known as Second-Wave Feminism. The film *The Sound of Music* appeared in 1965, six years after the Broadway play, which tells us not a lot had changed over those years.

Admittedly, the character Rolf—the mansplainer—does become a Nazi later in the script, but, unfortunately, mansplaining is not shown to be a factor in that decision.

Mansplaining. It's about speaking from a position of privilege. There's a Tumblr site, mansplained.tumblr.com, where incidents of mansplaining appear in all their florid glory. After I started searching, I found several words I hadn't run into before: "man-turuption," "man-turpreting," "bro-propriating" (or "bro-opting") when a man steals a woman's idea. (I should add parenthetically that studies indicate that women also interrupt women more often than they interrupt men.)

Mansplaining is not, unfortunately, a new phenomenon. Woman have been noticing this a long time. In the early twentieth century, Gertrude Stein said of the poet Ezra Pound, who was given to pontificating, "A village explainer, excellent if you were a village, but if you were not, not."

In the mid nineteenth century, feminist and Unitarian Margaret Fuller said, "I know now all the people worth knowing in America and I find no intellect comparable to my own." That's the problem, isn't it? One way out is for us to listen to each other, which I will get to, but there are broader hopeful signs I think.

The first idea I want to consider is that the mass society that developed in the Industrial Age—with its propensity toward hierarchy and mansplaining—is quickly coming to an end. (The fact that almost everyone here today has seen *The Sound of Music* is a mass culture phenomenon.) That clearly doesn't mean that human beings aren't living in mass groups. Cities are exploding in population and rural areas are thinning out all over the planet.

Yet, even as we live closer and closer together in bigger and bigger groups, technology allows us to break into smaller and smaller groups. Marketing guru Seth Godin calls this "the birth of weird."

This is perhaps most apparent in music. Before the 1920s, all music was live music. If you wanted to hear something by Bach, you had to travel to a place where Bach was being played or you had to be rich enough to hire musicians to come to you. Thomas Jefferson, for instance, famously hired servants based on their ability to play particular instruments.

Then, along came recording. Then radio.

By the 1940s in the US, radio and recordings had created a mass culture. For example, during the Second World War American sentries didn't need to learn passwords, because they could tell true-blue Americans by asking questions about the newest music on *Your Hit Parade* or about celebrities from radio programs or sports.

I, for one—were I asked anything about the popular music of today—would be immediately shot. And that's not only because I'm old; it's also because—like people of all ages—my Internet radio stations are based on my tastes and choices, not on the mass market. This multitude of choices allows what Seth Godin calls "weird."

The same thing is true of the news—we've got MSNBC people, and we've got Fox News people. Presumably the same events are occurring in everybody's world, but the media—the intermediaries we choose to give us the news—vary according to personal taste.

That's the death of mass culture and "the birth of weird." I don't remember the last time I listened to music on the radio. Playing recordings on the radio used to be my profession; and I'm glad I got out because I suspect there's not a lot of future in radio . . . at least not in playing the Top 40. That was mass culture. This, now, is weird.

Another example: two billion people on the planet are now on Facebook.

Or consider YouTube—three hundred hours of content is uploaded to YouTube... every minute of every day. Forget *Your Hit Parade* or the Top 40 playlist. There is now an "Official Independent Singles Chart Top 50." Mass culture, and its attendant assumptions of who is in and who is out of power and privilege, is fragmenting.

I subscribe to podcasts. My podcasts have to do with science and psychology. I hear about one podcast, and it leads to another. And all of them agree with my view of the world.

Yes, two billion people are on Facebook, but all two billion of us aren't seeing the same Facebook. Facebook appears in more than seventy languages, and counting. Some of us see a Facebook that's liberal; some see a Facebook that's conservative. Some of us read about the latest thing in science. Some of us read about the paranormal. And on and on—the birth of weird.

Clearly all this diversity does not spell the immediate doom of mansplaining, but it gives voice to marginalized people and gives us all opportunities to hear previously silent voices.

That's one bit of hope I see. The other is swarm theory.

Ants have been surviving on this planet for 140 million years. *Homo sapiens* for something around 200,000 years. Ants are doing something right, and what I think they've got right is cooperation.

Ants. Bees. We say that hives have queens, but actually, in the worlds of bees and ants, queens lay eggs; they don't boss anybody around. They don't have big expense accounts or big ideas. They don't read books on management theory.

There is no central authority, yet, day to day, ants get their working orders and get the job done. They change jobs, from nest repair to fighting to foraging.

Bees find where the pollen is and report back. They report on the direction of pollen and quantity and we don't know what all else.

The insight is that complex behaviors can occur without centralized control. *Homo sapiens* haven't lived that way. We've talked about chiefs and alpha males. And monarchy. We talk about power, political intrigue, and hierarchy. We've accepted mansplaining as the way thing have to be.

But those attitudes are beginning to change. We are using the insights that swarm theory is teaching—with the help of computers and big data—to plan automobile traffic patterns, air traffic, and electrical grids. We haven't even scratched the surface.

Dr. Thomas Seeley of Cornell University studies honey bees. He also happens to be the chair of the biology department. In order to stop the showboating, pontificating, posturing, and mansplaining that are traditional in academic situations, Dr. Seeley asks faculty members to think of as many solutions to a problem as they can—even solutions they don't agree with. Then, in the faculty meeting, people list the possibilities for solving a problem, without argument for or against any particular solution. They narrow down the choices, then the faculty votes by secret ballot.

Dr. Seeley says, "It's exactly what the swarm bees do, which gives a group time to let the best ideas emerge and win." Strong, bold mansplaining is simply not the way to solve problems. We don't need a mansplainer-in-chief. That goes for faculty. That goes for government and corporations. And it even holds true in congregations.

In other words, that old idea that democracy is the best way to make decisions may be correct. It's just that we have gotten the process wrong. We don't need to elect a mansplainer-in-chief. We need to get as wide a variety of input and opinion and expertise as possible. We need to stop the showboating and start listening to each other.

Now to the personal: that scenario of mansplaining we saw in the Rogers and Hammerstein song is how a lot of ugly oppression happens in our world, isn't it? It's up close and personal.

This 'splaining stuff is about privilege and power: I'm right *because* I'm the man. I'm right *because* I'm White. I'm right *because* I'm rich. I'm right because . . . I have a master's degree in science!

White-splaining. Straight-splaining. Middle-class-splaining. All of these are saying, "You have to listen to me explain. I will explain away social inequalities; I will explain how what you are doing is a bad idea. You don't know what you're doing with Black Lives Matter because . . ."

All of these 'splainings are saying, "Hey, female, brown, queer, working-class people, count your lucky stars: it's *so much better* than it used to be." You don't know what you're doing with Black Lives Matter because "it's *so much better* than it used to be." All of those 'splainers are singing a little song:

> Totally unprepared are you
> To face a world of "older, straight, White" men
> Timid and shy and scared are you
> Of things beyond your ken—

"You just don't understand how things are, oppressed person. Allow me to explain."

Writer Rebecca Solnit in her book *Men Explain Things to Me* says,

> Men explain things to me, still. And no man has ever apologized for explaining, wrongly, things that I know and they don't. Not yet, but according to the actuarial tables, I may have another forty-something years to live, more or less, so it could happen. Though I'm not holding my breath.

What is the cost to humanity of this kind of day-to-day oppression? In the essay where this quote appears, Solnit tells a story about getting mansplained to by a guy quoting facts from a book that she wrote.

Fact is, all of us here today are privileged in some ways and oppressed in others. Besides gender and color, there's how old you are, how much you weigh, if you're in a wheelchair . . . if you're a theist or an a-theist . . . the list just goes on and on.

Following this logic, finally we reach the bottom of a long, slippery slope, where none of us can speak for or to another—I'm only a White heterosexual farmer from the Midwest, and a baby boomer, so what can I say?

What we can do is listen. We can listen, whether that's with our two good ears, or our hearing-aided ears, or in American Sign Language. We can listen to each other. We can realize the validity of lived experience. We can encourage people to tell their stories.

The question becomes how we speak our own truths, realizing all the while that those truths are partial readings of a much larger and longer story—the human story. We must strive to think outside of the sociological categories we are born into and toward deeper and more universal human truths.

We owe it to ourselves and each other to respect the "inherent worth and dignity of every person." To work toward democratic systems in which all voices are heard. Lofty goals—but Ralph Waldo Emerson cautioned long ago, "Use what language you will, you can never say anything but what you are." Then, perhaps, the lyrics become:

> Totally prepared are you
> To live in the Black, queer, gender ambiguous, immigrant, working-class world—
> You're not timid, shy, or scared
> And you know what you know . . .

Seriously—Who Said We Can Choose Our Own Mysteries?

There is more than one type of mystery. Some mysteries aren't even mysterious. For example, how a diesel engine works is a mystery to many, but only to those who haven't taken the time to study diesel engines. They are a marvel of complexity, yes. But there's no mystery to how a diesel engine works. People design them. People build them. People repair them.

How planes fly, how battle ships float, how cereal stays fresh for months in cardboard boxes . . . none of these are mysteries to those who bother to look into them and figure out how they work.

Then there are those things that once were mysteries but aren't any longer. How Ouija boards work, for example, isn't a mystery. The motions are due to the "ideomotor effect." That's the term that scientist William Carpenter coined in 1882 when he was researching how fortune-telling pendulums and dowsing rods work.

Carpenter also studied the movements of tables at séances. No, the movers and shakers are not spirits. They are us, ourselves. We don't even know it, Carpenter argued, but we unconsciously make the movements we expect spirits or magic magnetic forces to make.

How dowsing rods work is not a mystery either.

But the reason that Ouija boards are not a mystery is that curiosity led someone to discover the truth. Fact is, the ideomotor effect is counter to the evidence of our own senses: we don't know we are producing the movements that we think are coming from the spirit world. Our senses have fooled us.

Only a deep curiosity to solve a mystery can lead to this kind of discovery. This is the distinction I'm searching for. Mystery, it appears, can lead to complacence and even superstition, or it can lead to discovery.

That's why the battle between science and religion has been so brutal for so long in the Western world. It has been twenty-five hundred years since Socrates was convicted for "refusing to recognize the gods acknowledged by the state, and importing strange divinities of his own."[1]

---

1. The death sentence of Socrates, as cited in Whitmarsh, *Battling the Gods*.

After the Bloody Mary Game

Can the gods make rain if there are no clouds? Socrates thought it's not likely. His assertion threatened to kill a sacred cow. Yet slowly, over time, more and more people looked at the mystery of rain and decided that perhaps the phenomenon occurred for some reason other than the actions of the gods.

It makes me wonder why the Abrahamic monotheisms—Judaism, Christianity, and Islam—have been so resistant to scientific knowledge while Hinduism, Buddhism, Confucianism, Daoism, and Earth-based religions have not. Is that another one of those mysteries?

Is this resistance to science a product of these particular religions, or is it a product of the ways of thinking that led to these religions? After all, Socrates died four hundred years before the birth of Jesus, but both were killed by the state. Could it be that democracy is the problem? Or perhaps patriarchal rule? Or perhaps the very oppression itself served to encourage curiosity?

Is it a mystery? I'm curious.

We human beings have a sense of awe and wonder that motivates us to ask questions, that motivates us to use our imaginations and our reason. At one time, a time before microscopes and telescopes and oscilloscopes and scoping in general, stories and reason were all we had. Then we began to build instruments. Eventually we figured out why it rains. How do we answer some of those other mysteries, questions such as:

> What is the purpose of the universe?
> Why are we here?
> What is the purpose of our lives?
> Who's in charge here?

For many people, even those living in the industrialized world, the answers to these questions remain steadfastly in the realm of superstition.

Who's in charge here? El? Yahweh? Astarte? Quetzalcoatl? Vucub-Caquix? (a Mayan bird god). Gods and gods in charge of this and that, gods in human form, gods in animal form. For human beings at one time, stories were all we had. Eventually a curious Greek named Xenophanes came along and said,

> If oxen and horses and lions had hands and were able to draw with
> their hands and do the same things as we do, horses would draw
> the shapes of gods to look like horses and oxen would draw them

to look like oxen, and each would make the gods' bodies have the same shape as they themselves had.

Xenophanes—he was roughly a contemporary of Socrates—saw that our stories concerning these ultimate questions depend upon anthropomorphism. We create gods in our own image. They do things that we understand. "Why would that be?," asked Xenophanes. It was a mystery.

Seriously: What is the purpose of the universe?

Xenophanes told us, twenty-five hundred years ago: even if there were a purpose, human beings would not understand it. Purpose is an anthropomorphism, a giving the universe human characteristics. We might as well ask, "Does the universe yearn? Does the universe get hungry?"

Xenophanes remains today, as skeptical as ever, whispering into our ears: the universe just isn't human, even if we imagine a really, really big human. Poet Dana Gioia expresses this in a poem called "Words":

> The world does not need words. It articulates itself
> in sunlight, leaves, and shadows. The stones on the path
> are no less real for lying uncatalogued and uncounted.
> The fluent leaves speak only the dialect of pure being.

The purpose of the universe in relation to human beings is not a mystery: the universe does not need us and our endless words. As Ludwig Wittgenstein said, "If a lion could talk, we could not understand him."

There. That is where the mystery is. Because we need purpose, we project purpose upon the universe. Our first job is to figure out that we do that. And then stop doing that.

Only then can we get down to a real mystery: each of us can ask ourselves, "What is my purpose?" When each of us figures that out, we have pursued wisdom and caught up with it. Maybe even put a saddle on it for awhile.

Wisdom is knowing that I, you, all of us—nobody has a purpose . . . until we figure it out. And, even after we do manage to wrestle it to the ground and put a bridle on it once, our purpose is very likely to do a little Houdini on us. Purpose is a shape shifter, if you will. It's a moving target in our lives.

Our own purpose is the greatest mystery. Yet, we know we've got it when we feel the excitement of living in this world. As Howard Thurman famously said, "Don't ask what the world needs. Ask what makes you come alive, and go do it. Because what the world needs is people who have come alive."

Seriously: who said we get to declare our own mysteries? The age of the Earth is not a mystery. When dinosaurs existed is not a mystery. That natural selection shaped life on this planet is not a mystery.

Just because I don't know something—from ignorance, lack of will, or even adamant refusal to see the facts—does not make it a mystery. As science fiction writer Philip K. Dick put it, "Reality is that which, when you stop believing in it, doesn't go away."

Our challenge in this world is not to create mysteries that are not there. Our challenge is to adjust to the real. And to find our meaning and our purpose in the here and now—here and now, which is all we have and all we will ever have.

Theoretical physicist Max Planck said, "Science cannot solve the ultimate mystery of nature. And that is because, in the last analysis, we ourselves are a part of the mystery that we are trying to solve."

Yes, that's how it is.

Love Thy Neighbor as . . .

I spent some time in the hospital with sciatica. It's a spinal thing. A nerve gets pinched. And it hurts like heck. I'm not one of those who views suffering as good for the soul, but the experience certainly reminded me about humility and how important it is to have others come to your aid.

My attack manifested itself by paralyzing my left side from my waist down. Then there's the pain—it's like having a charley horse that lasts for something like forty-eight hours. When the attack became unbearable, I called 911. My wife had already left for work. So, the paramedics came and had to break open the door because I couldn't move. That started my little journey.

The staff of my congregation jumped into action. I was scheduled to speak at another pulpit that Sunday. One of my assistant ministers volunteered to do that, and she drove there and read the talk that I had prepared. Though I spent weeks on oxycodone and couldn't drive, I was able to conduct most of my day-to-day chores with the help of the wonderful staff and volunteers in the congregation.

Saying that it takes a village is not the half of it. The conventionally religious often ask me if humanists have a concept of grace, as in "god shed his grace on thee." I always reply—and I can reply even more emphatically after my experience last weekend—that grace for me is the fact that most of the time human beings will go out of their way to help. *Way* out of their way to help.

There are these things that we call virtues: empathy, compassion, courage, generosity, fairness, loyalty. Virtues, but those words are mere abstractions until they are made concrete in our actions daily and hourly. Think what human beings are capable of: all those virtues I mentioned, but so much more—love, creativity, music, altruism, generosity, forgiveness, spontaneity, ethics, aesthetics. Philosophy.

Furthermore, these are human virtues that cross all of the artificial boundaries we create and take too seriously, from the gender binary to race, class, and nationalism. These virtues also cross religious barriers; both the religious and irreligious share these virtues. It appears from the evidence that both our virtues and many of our taboos are the result of human nature rather than religious imposition. To which I have to say, "How cool is that?"

When I was in my twenties I began searching for something deeper than the religion I had grown up with. I was looking for a religion or philosophy that talked more explicitly about virtues than the Christianity I grew up with was capable of doing.

You remember the story. It occurs in the Gospel of Luke, chapter 10. A young lawyer comes to talk with Jesus and asks how he can achieve salvation. The answer Jesus gives is, "Love God and love your neighbor." The young lawyer asks, "Who is my neighbor?" Jesus responds with one of the great stories of human civilization—the story of the Good Samaritan. The answer Jesus gives is much like the answer Mr. Rogers gives: everyone, everywhere is your neighbor.

I took this story to heart as a young person. And the disjunction between that liberal, humanist story that Jesus tells and the very exclusionary and judgmental faith that I grew up in is the reason I went looking for a new religion.

As I searched, I was drawn to Buddhism for a couple of reasons. One reason was that the Beats, better known as Beatnicks, whose poetry I admired, were for the most part Buddhists. Secondly, upon reading into Buddhism, I discovered that the focus of Buddhism is compassion for not just human beings or even only animals, but, as the Buddhists say, "all sentient beings."

•

I think these words from Yongey Mingyur Rinpoche are a perfect example of what drew me to Buddhism:

> Once we recognize that other sentient beings—people, animals, and even insects—are just like us, that their basic motivation is to experience peace and to avoid suffering, then when someone acts in some way or says something that is against our wishes, we're able to have some basis for understanding: "Oh, well, this person (or whatever) is coming from this position because, just like me, they want to be happy and they want to avoid suffering. That's their basic purpose. They're not out to get me; they're only doing what they think they need to do.

However we get ourselves there—religion, philosophy, meditation—that's the place I'm convinced that we all need to be.

And it's not just that there's this big "ought to" or this big "should." I'm convinced that *that* place of compassion is also the place we *yearn* to be: knowing "that other sentient beings—people, animals, and even insects—are just like us, that their basic motivation is to experience peace and to avoid suffering." I think that place of big compassion is where we naturally are *when* we get out of our own way and listen to that self we have beyond all the ego. That place is our happy place, if you will. Our inner *Mister Roger's Neighborhood*.

That place—compassion—goes beyond "loving thy neighbor as thyself" and leads toward a deeper understanding, and another of the great Buddhist insights: actually, your neighbor *is* yourself. And that bird is yourself. And that spider is yourself. And that tree is yourself. That's what the great religions teach. That's what transcendentalism taught back in the days of Emerson and Thoreau. And it's what humanism teaches today. It came to Charles Darwin in a flash and he wrote it in his notebook: "We all may be netted together."

This compassion springs from the fact that all things are temporary—from our own lives to the Earth itself—that all the things we see here, today, will be gone, part of the flow of the universe. Buddhism teaches two truths: that all things go away, and that we must have compassion for all those things that are here, now. The purported last words of the Buddha were, "Everything changes. Nothing lasts. Keep going."

We live a shared life in a shared world. And our shared lives and our shared world are all about change and loss. What we have is each other, because that impulse toward sharing is what love means. It's the only hope for humanity's survival.

Language, Love, and Capability

Back in 1995, a relationship councilor named Gary Chapman published a book called *The Five Love Languages: How to Express Heartfelt Commitment to Your Mate*. Chapman came up with five ways people express love. He lists gifts, quality time, words of affirmation, acts of service (devotion), and physical touch (intimacy).

Chapman's idea has been used and adapted into several relationship counseling programs. The love languages concept is useful because it explicitly cautions against "loving thy neighbor as thyself." For example, those who see love as a desire to share quality time will feel unloved by a partner who expresses love through gift giving. Both partners are being equally sincere, but the partner who wants quality time and gets gifts will sooner or later say, "All you ever do is get me stuff; I want your time."

It's not enough to love thy neighbor as thyself. You must love your neighbor as your neighbor needs to be loved. This requires getting outside your own head and really perceiving another person as an individual with needs and desires that may not match your own. This is the way we get from empathy—which is merely realizing that another person has needs—to compassion, in which we actively wish to discover what those needs are and fulfill them if we can.

Martha Nussbaum is a philosopher who has done groundbreaking work on what she calls "capabilities." She works with people in various cultures trying to make their lives better, but, rather than using the usual Western model of sweeping in and trying to turn, say, poor women in India into middle-class American women, Nussbaum says that we must study what the capabilities of the people in a particular setting are, given the social and political realities that shape their lives.

Thus, for example, many disadvantaged women in India need a way to escape from the virtual prison that arranged marriages can be. Yet, the idea of romantic love is not popular in India, so women who escape a bad marriage are not likely to be remarried. Leaving a marriage means leaving the basic social structure of Indian society. Given the social pressures and assumptions of that place, what are the capabilities of these women? What can be done to help them have better lives? We can't love those neighbors as ourselves—we must love them as they need to be loved . . .

Loving your neighbor as yourself is not a one-size-fits-all deal. We've got to get outside our own assumptions and biases and blind spots. There's an old Buddhist story that goes like this:

> Once a mother found her baby extremely ill. She was afraid it would die. She had heard that the Buddha was teaching nearby, so she grabbed tip her baby and rushed to the Buddha to ask that her baby be healed.
>
> "Why do you want your baby healed?" the Buddha asked.
>
> The mother was aghast: "because my baby is suffering and I'm afraid! This is a tragedy!"
>
> The Buddha said, "I will heal your child. All I ask is that you return to your village, and knock at every door until you find a household where there has been no tragedy. When you find that house, ask for a handful of rice and bring it back to me."
>
> So the mother rushed into the village and began knocking on doors. "Have you experience a tragedy?" she asked. "Have you experienced a tragedy?" She ran from door to door hoping to collect that handful of rice but found that every house had experienced a tragedy of some sort—disease, hunger, poverty . . .
>
> The mother returned to the Buddha and said, "I see. I understand." And she went home with her child.

Compare that story to the Christian narrative of Jesus healing the sick, and I think we get at the basic difference between Buddhism and Christianity. And we get at what drew me to the compassion that Buddhism teaches. It would be grand were we to get our own personal miracles every time we asked for one. But that's a fairy tale. If those sorts of miracles occurred, who among us would be sick or old of depressed? Who among us would have lost our parents or siblings or loved ones?

Compassion involves the understanding that there's nothing unique about me, me, me. We all lead a shared life in a shared world. No one ever asked us to like it. Yet, to find any happiness at all, we've got to adjust to what reality looks like—and it looks like everything keeps changing.

When I was tossing and turning in agony at the hospital, I would certainly have taken a personal miracle. But there's a phrase I've seldom heard a humanist utter: "Why me?"

Because humanism puts you in that place where the mother in the old Buddhist story is, realizing that suffering is the human condition. When we think otherwise, we merely haven't noticed the pain and tragedy our neighbors have been facing because we've been too caught up in our own stuff.

Humanism is here to tell us that we are already whole and complete and OK. Like everything else in the universe, we are the products of laws and forces. That's the good news. The bad news is that everything in the universe is changing all the time.

While I sat with my dying father, I both wanted his suffering to be over and hoped he wouldn't die now. Those two emotions are primal but are irreconcilable. I don't have any easy out to suggest. We have those two systems that psychologist Danial Kahnaman talks about, "thinking fast" and "thinking slow." That is, our immediate emotional response and our slow, reasoned response. Only my reasoned response kept me focused as my father died. I didn't expect a miracle and I didn't ask "Why me?"

What would have been the point? Crying "Why me, why me, why me?" is simply egotism and arrogance. As the Aristotle quipped, "Luck is when the arrow hits the guy next to you."

Humanism does not argue with reality. Naturally, all of us would love to change reality. We know better than to argue, however. Yongey Mingyur Rinpoche's words ring true:

> Compassion is the spontaneous wisdom of the heart. It's always with us. It always has been and always will be. When it arises in us, we've simply learned to see how strong and safe we really are.

Then we know from the evidence that the Buddha had it right: "Everything changes. Nothing lasts. Keep going."

Fallen Angels, Rising Apes, and the Knowledge of the Serpent

In addition to the Unitarian Universalist Seven Principles, the congregation that I serve as minister ascribes to a set of aspirational statements that are specifically humanist. Our first aspiration is, "To live joyfully and ethically, in loving, reverent relationship with humanity and nature."

Why do we say such a thing? Because we are countering a long tradition of life-denying dogma common in the Western world. Doctrines such as original sin are not affirmations of life in this world, which in our view is the only life there is.

You don't have to go further than the congregation's bulletin board to see an implication of what we mean. Just now we have a poster advocating "sex-positive reproductive justice." We are countering a culture in which sex-negative attitudes impact the fundamental rights of women.

Dostoyevsky saw free will this way: "One's own free unfettered choice, one's own caprice, however wild it may be, one's own fancy worked up at times to frenzy . . ."

Well, it's certainly "joyful" to do "one's own fancy," but such actions may not meet the ethical or "reverent relationship" criterion. Dostoyevsky's definition of free will—the freedom to really mess things up—is a negative assertion of freedom. There's always the poles: sex-negative; sex-positive. Freedom-negative; freedom-positive. Navigating those can be problematic. And traditional Western religions are not a solution but the problem.

In Dostoyevsky's time philosophers were grappling with the implications of the discovery by Joseph Fourier, a French mathematician, that the numbers of births, deaths, house fires, and crimes—and even the types of crimes—proved to be consistent from year to year. Predictable, in other words.

This insight led to both the insurance industry and the field of sociology, among other things. My inability to diet and the number of people who die of heart attack and stroke each year in the United States has some connection, now, doesn't it?

The insurance industry certainly sees a connection.

Unlike in Dostoyevsky's time, we don't think much about it nowadays when we hear how many Americans will die of type 2 diabetes or high blood pressure this year. Nowadays we are saturated with statistics. So much so that, with the addition of computers, we live in the next iteration of statistical analysis: "big data" or "predictive analytics."

Netflix can tell us what movies we will enjoy with a high degree of accuracy. Amazon can send us discounts for things that the crunched data indicate we will consume next. I love a sentence I read about predictive analytics: "Analytical Customer Relationship Management can be applied throughout the customer's lifecycle."

Think about that: "Analytical Customer Relationship Management can be applied throughout the customer's lifecycle."

So when you start getting coupons for caskets . . . watch out.

It makes me want to go Dostoyevsky's route and buy something *really* crazy.

Looked at from this angle, Dostoyevsky wasn't defining free will; he was defining actions that do not take others into account: "One's own free unfettered choice, one's own caprice . . . one's own fancy worked up at times to frenzy . . ."

•

One of the oddest things I have to deal with in multifaith work is answering the accusation that humanists don't have a "theology of sin." As in, "You don't have a theology of sin, therefore . . . you're just not all that serious about living right, are you?"

To which I'm tempted to say that humanism doesn't have a unique theory of onomatopoeia either.

It's not that humanists don't understand what people are talking about when they discuss onomatopoeia; it's just that it lies outside the purview of a humanist ethic.

It's simply that I don't put any credence in the idea that people are born into a "fallen state." As far as I can see, a "theology of sin" has a lot of baggage that just has nothing to do with describing reality. It's a complicated answer to a simple question: Why do people act like animals?" When St. Augustine came up with his theory of original sin, people didn't know that human beings are animals. (Call it self-denial.) But now we do.

How could an animal that has evolved a consciousness such as we have be "fallen"? I think anthropologist Robert Ardrey put it best:

> We were born of risen apes, not fallen angels, and the apes were armed killers besides.[1]

Claiming that "original sin" is not a true description of reality is in no way saying that human beings are born good.

Original sin is a theological concept that serves theological ends. And it is a complex answer to a simple question that does not survive an application of Occam's razor.

There's nothing original about sin. But there is something very original about acting up to human aspirations toward ethics and compassion. We are "risen apes, not fallen angels," and we are "armed killers besides." That is a considerably clearer place to begin considering how to be ethical, loving, and reverent, it seems to me.

Allow me to take a crack at a humanist theology of sin, necessarily taking into account evolution. How about this: "sin" is a failure to cooperate.

Excessive drinking, smoking, eating too much—these aren't sins. They're merely really bad behaviors, given what we know about their outcomes. Those seven deadly sins—wrath, greed, sloth, pride, lust, envy, gluttony—they're bad for the self and they are often bad for others.

"We were born of risen apes, not fallen angels, and the apes were armed killers besides." Too often our reason and creativity has been used to invent sharpened sticks . . . and a few other things to kill each other with. This is "sin": it is a lack of cooperation and compassion for others.

That tale of the Garden of Eden is a good story, but it has led to some bad behavior. Our challenge is to look reality in the face and do what we can with what we've got.

Sin isn't very original.

Allow me to take another shot at a humanist theory of sin:

Some things, such as what have been called sins, are the default settings on the human body. The out-of-the-box model, so to speak. But every car enthusiast knows that if you want more performance, you've got to get yourself an after-market muffler. Human ethics are like that.

Aspirations toward living ethically, in loving, reverent relationship with humanity and nature are mostly aftermarket add-ons.

Okay. So I know that my metaphor doesn't have the sizzle of two naked people and a talking snake. (That's good writing!) Still, my metaphor is truer to the human condition.

---

1. Ardrey, *African Genesis*.

We are "risen apes, not fallen angels." We are prone to unoriginal appetites, irresponsibility, uncooperativeness, and killing. Still, we can aspire to live joyfully and ethically, in loving, reverent relationship with humanity and nature.

Not bad for a bunch of primates.

3

Where Does Humanism Come From?

Humanism, Like Mushrooms

When primates began to look at the stars in wonder, humanism was born. Far from the cliché of superstitious creatures huddled in caves, *Homo sapiens* have from the beginning been engineers and artists, philosophers and scientists discovering how to adapt to our environment and make the most of our brief time on the planet.

Humanists then and now ask a question: What are we to do with the life that we have? The humanist difference is that we do not accept ready-made answers. The ideas and ideals of humanism have sprouted in many times and places.

Among animals, human beings are unique in that we have developed methods to conceptualize time and ways to preserve and communicate knowledge and culture across generations. Humanity evolved complex social relationships and unique solutions to complex challenges, yet we are also prone to superstitions and hatreds—aspects of ourselves that must be transcended.

Humanist ideas are universal in scope and continuous through time, anywhere an inquiring mind has met an intractable problem or mystery. Rather than accepting the easy answers, humanists never stop asking why and how. Humanists are the empiricists, the questioners, the artists who push knowledge to the edge, then press on.

Chinese Daoism, probably the oldest continuously practiced human religion, teaches observation and acceptance of the nature of reality as the highest good.

The Charvaka movement developed in India in the 600s BCE and appears to have been the earliest philosophy to embrace skepticism and reason in matters of belief. The Charvakas dismissed the supernatural and embraced a materialist, observational stance. These lines summarize their humanist stance which rejected the supernatural and an afterlife:

> While life is yours live joyously;
> No one can avoid Death's searching eye:
> When this body of ours is burnt,
> How can it ever return again?

Like many humanists, both the Indian philosopher Gautama Buddha (c. 563–480 BCE) and the Chinese philosopher Confucius (551–479 BCE) did not deny the existence of the gods of their cultures, but they did dismiss theological questions as irrelevant to living a meaningful life.

Though its origins are lost, Jainism is non-theistic and teaches liberation though human effort.

The Greek philosopher Protagoras (490–420 BCE) said, "Man is the measure of all things." Like many since, Plato worked very hard to disprove this by asserting an intelligence beyond the material world. Protagoras insisted, "As touching the gods, I do not know whether they exist or not, nor how they look; for there is much to prevent our knowing—the obscurity of the subject and the brevity of human life."

The Chinese philosopher Mozi (470–391 BCE) asked:

> What is the purpose of houses? It is to protect us from the wind and cold of winter, the heat and rain of summer, and to keep out robbers and thieves. Once these ends have been secured, that is all. Whatever does not contribute to these ends should be eliminated.

This going back to basics has long been a humanist ideal. Mozi also said, "Universal love is really the way of the sage-kings. It is what gives peace to the rulers and sustenance to the people." Like most humanists today, Mozi condemned both war and the death penalty:

> The murder of one person is called unrighteous and incurs one death penalty. Following this argument, the murder of ten persons will be ten times as unrighteous and there should be ten death penalties; the murder of a hundred persons will be a hundred times as unrighteous and there should be a hundred death penalties. All the gentlemen of the world know that they should condemn these things, calling them unrighteous. But when it comes to the great unrighteousness of attacking states, they do not know that they should condemn it. On the contrary, they applaud it, calling it righteous.

Where Does Humanism Come From?

No one knows for sure how long the humanist tradition of *ubuntu* has existed in Africa. *Ubuntu* means "I am well if you are well." Desmond Tutu says of Ubuntu,

> You can't be human all by yourself, and when you have this quality—Ubuntu—you are known for your generosity. We think of ourselves far too frequently as just individuals, separated from one another, whereas you are connected and what you do affects the whole World.

This impulse has led humanists to embrace the United Nations Universal Declaration of Human Rights.

The book called Ecclesiastes, among the scriptures of both Judaism and Christianity and written sometime around 300 BCE, reflects rationality and skepticism. The text assumes there is no afterlife and that living well in the face of endless cycles of time—"There is nothing new under the sun"—is the only viable choice for humanity.

The philosopher Epicurus (341–270 BCE) wrote, "Rejecting the popular myths does not make one impious; preaching them is what demonstrates impiety." Epicurus rejected myths and sought truth. He may not have written the following lines—that is debatable—but the idea is Epicurean:

> Is god willing to prevent evil but not able?
> Then he is not all-powerful.
> Is he able, but not willing?
> Then where does evil come from?
> Is he neither able nor willing?
> When why call him god?

The Epicurean and Stoic philosophers of the Greek and Roman Empires were proponents of reason and observers of nature. Epicurus said, "Our deepest fears remain until we understand the nature of the universe rather than trusting one myth or another. Peace of mind requires the study of reality."

As with the Charvakas, who reached their conclusions based on Hindu thought, the Mutazilites were a rational group that arose in Islam beginning in the eighth century CE.

Sumak kawsay, or "the good life," is a contemporary popularization of the ancient wisdom of indigenous South American peoples. The focus of the movement is saving our biosphere from rampant development.

The Western literary and artistic tradition, later studied in the university curriculum as the humanities, also encouraged humanist thinking.

The nineteenth-century French philosopher August Comte was apparently the first to realize that church could be done without reference to religion. He worked at creating what he called the "religion of humanity." Comte's motto was *ivre pour autrui*, "live for others," from which we derive the term "altruism." Altruism remains an ideal of humanism.

Comte was the direct inspiration for Felix Adler, founder of the Ethical Society, and John Dietrich, founder of the Unitarian Humanist tradition.

Philosopher Alain de Botton founded an "atheist church" in London in the early twenty-first century, soon to be followed by Sunday Assemblies, with franchises in several cities around the world.

There is no patent on the concept of humanism, nor is there any lack of creativity among those seeking community outside of traditional religious concepts and institutions.

The essential is to take a hard look at form and function. Traditional religions take many forms in their congregational gatherings. What, however, is the function? Do assumptions about the supernatural in any way change that function?

Humanist thought stretches across time and space. Humanists live in the observable world. Twentieth-century Unitarian Curtis Reese once said of the idea of God, "philosophically possible, scientifically unproved, and religiously unnecessary." That is the humanist life stance.

You will know humanists because we do not worship, nor do we pray, nor do we bow before the ideas, idols, or ideologies of our fellow *Homo sapiens*. We live as global citizens in the cosmos. In awe, gratitude, and hope, humanists know that we are one with all. We dedicate our lives to healing the planet and freeing humanity.

Three Decorating Ideas for the Mind
(or Making Sense of Life)

Poet Wallace Stevens once said, "How full of trifles everything is! It is only one's thoughts that fill a room with something more than furniture." At first glance, this perhaps sounds like a Disneyesque reflection on the uses of a hearty imaginal life. Or—since Stevens was a poet—a reflection on the power of metaphor to set solid things flying.

At second glance—since Stevens was both a poet and an atheist—perhaps it is a reflection on what he saw as the most fruitful power in the universe: the human mind's power to construct meaning as we go along in an otherwise material and un-human universe.

Most likely, Stevens meant all these things and more. After all, his poems sport beautiful and improbable and impermanent "furniture" such as peacocks, round jars in Tennessee, and emperors of ice cream. Stevens also wrote of "the palm at the end of the mind." Yes, the palm is a tropical tree. It is also the human hand, our hands. We ourselves are the end of meaning ... because we are the only creatures in the world that reach for something called meaning, at least something called "human meaning."

Moment to moment we are faced with a question: How do I make sense of my life? "It is only one's thoughts that fill a room," Stevens wrote, "with something more than furniture." And it is only one's thoughts that fill a universe full of furniture with meaning.

Religions (and the lack thereof) reflect the values of the cultures in which they develop. Religions (and their lack) serve as both a reflection of the aspirations of particular groups and also as guides for individuals within a group when we may be in doubt concerning what our culture and our religious belief or non-belief requires of us. Religions also fill the room with more than furniture: they help us make sense of our lives.

Pragmatist philosophers claim that labeling one truth as "true" and another as "false" doesn't reveal much. It is more useful to see all views—religious and otherwise—as devices to get results. After all, if beliefs did not get results, they would not survive the test of time. The question—at least for those who are free enough of theocracy to have a choice—is: Which of the many ways of seeing produce the most desirable results; which ways of seeing make the most sense out of our lives.

Is it somehow useful for making sense of life, for instance, to believe that Fridays which fall on the thirteenth of the month have special properties?

Over time human beings have posited two very different views of how the world works. One view is that the order we see is the order that is: sure, we will keep discovering more and more about that order, but it's all out there to observe, albeit some of it observable only with a large hadron collider.

The opposite view (the opposite "truth") is that there is a higher order not discoverable by observation. This is usually accompanied by speculation concerning a god or gods, though it doesn't have to. (For example, the Renaissance-era belief in alchemy did not require gods in order to function, even though that belief system existed in parallel to Christianity.)

These polar opposites are not always opposite in practice. Many otherwise "materialist" people leave room for "powers unseen," as the *Book of Common Prayer* would have it. Be that as it may, there is a great gulf fixed between those who trust observation to reveal "truth" and those who depend up the revelation of sacred texts and seers of various sorts, be they prophets or gurus.

Wallace Stevens was on the side of observation. He found the most reliable way to get results was to posit a lack of meaning (at least human meaning) beyond the human mind and its creative interaction with the furniture of the universe.

Is there a difference between the words of Moses and the words of Wallace Stevens? Stevens thought not. Sure, some poets and some poems are better at filling rooms with more than furniture, and large hadron colliders can rewrite all we know about the room and the furniture. Yet, in essence, it's all about the human imagination. It's up to us to animate the room with sense and meaning.

We ourselves are the end of (human) meaning . . . because we are the only creatures in the world that can imagine something called (human) meaning. Moment to moment we are faced with a question: How do I make sense of my life? That room of creative experience is an entertaining place to live. As Stevens put it,

> A gold-feathered bird
> Sings in the palm, without human meaning,
> Without human feeling, a foreign song.

What Do Death Cults Really Want?

An *Atlantic* article by Graeme Wood, "What ISIS Really Wants," examines the ISIS phenomenon from the vantage point of apocalyptic movements. It's an insightful article. I'm just a bit confused at the reaction or surprise to the article. We've had apocalyptic thinking living in our midst here in the US for some time. I grew up Pentecostal. Now that's a death cult for you.

I grew up among people obsessed by "the end times" and obsessed with the thought that we were living in the end times. Preachers preached that each new headline proved that the time was short; that Jesus was coming back any moment now. The walls of my Sunday school were plastered with garish posters with fire and blood so that I could visualize the end of the world. Many in my family studied the signs of the times—talking, voting, expecting—for forty, fifty years . . . then died before any other kind of "end times" arrived.

I expect that I too will die long before the end of time.

For many Americans, the words in the book of Revelation remain both a frightening prospect and an excuse to do nothing for humanity or for our Earth.

When someone named John, sometime around the year 95 of the Common Era, wrote Revelation, he (or perhaps they) was already late in a long line of writers imagining the end of the world. And the tradition continues—the Left Behind franchise of books having toted up something over $700 million in sales.

The End is a growth industry. It fuels the murderous dreams of ISIS. And many Americans.

Admit it: there is an attractive aspect to thinking that you might see the whole sky roll up like a giant scroll. Our inner child wants the world to end in a grand sort of way before we ourselves end. We want God to put an end to this world so that we ourselves beat the odds and don't have to go the way of all flesh, ending like every other human being who has ever lived.

But that's the inner child talking; that is delusion speaking. Bad psychology, confused theology. Bad politics.

The fact is that the sort of eschatological thinking that has become so popular in the US is—contrary to what fundamentalists and evangelicals like to think—very new theology. The book of Revelation has long been held in suspicion in the Christian tradition. The Eastern Orthodox Church does not read Revelation as part of its yearly lectionary readings. In the Western Roman Catholic tradition, Revelation very nearly didn't make the final cut of what made it into Christian scripture.

For centuries, Revelation did not cut much of a figure. It took the poverty and violence of the American South to really get the end times rolling.

But there is a problem with this sort of thinking: the end doesn't come—not the wild screaming hordes of Gog and Magog signaling Armageddon, not the Four Horsemen of the Apocalypse, not Quetzalcoatl, not a golden age of political peace and prosperity, not the dreams of ISIS. This old world just keeps rolling along. And that's the real challenge we face.

In the Sutta Nipata, one of the oldest Buddhist manuscripts, written down somewhere around 200 BCE, we hear these words:

> What people expect to happen is always different from what actually happens.
> From this comes great disappointment; this is the way the world works.

Oh dear, don't you hate it when reality comes knocking?

Buffering for Fun and Profit

I'm from the southern part of Illinois, the bit of the Ozarks that brushes across the southern part of the state at the confluence of the Mississippi, Ohio, and Wabash Rivers. I'm a cracker.

My father's parents were sharecroppers—yes, that institution existed north of the Mason-Dixon line, just as slavery had. Slavery also existed in the southern part of the state—Illinois was the worst offender in the "reverse" underground railroad portrayed in the film *Ten Years a Slave*.

The first military victory of General Ulysses S. Grant was the occupation of southern Illinois to prevent the region from joining the Confederacy. We who have been there several generations have Southern roots, and we have not forgotten those roots.

My parents both grew up on subsistence farms in the southern part of Illinois before the days of electricity or running water. They were born two miles from each other but didn't meet until they were in the twenties.

My parents qualified as what philosopher Charles Taylor calls "porous selves"—the sort of people for whom life itself is as "authentic" and "real" as anybody could want. So real and authentic that they have to seek the supernatural in a desperate grasp for comfort and hope.

As Charles Taylor puts it, "The porous self is vulnerable: to spirits, demons, cosmic forces. And along with this go certain fears that can grip it in certain circumstances." Porous people are poor people, people walking life's tightrope without a social safety net.

Taylor contrasts this condition to the "buffered self"—people with connections, expectations, and networks. Taylor claims that the buffered self has escaped the world of this kind of fear.

When I talk about economic justice, it's personal: I know the cost of living and dying, as my father died with a sixth-grade education, and as my mother is illiterate. They were their whole lives "porous selves," victims of superstition, poverty, and exploitation.

Conversely, the "buffered self," according to Charles Taylor, often becomes secular, or at least "believes" in received religions only insofar as it chooses. For the most part, buffered selves consume other products of the culture instead of religion. Buffered people are free enough, in other words, from the fear of looming, immanent privation and death to—if they (we) choose—begin examining cultural assumptions, including one's religious ideas. If they choose.

I hasten to add that my parents did not see themselves as victims. They were part of that "greatest generation," who transitioned from growing and killing everything they ate to getting food in grocery stores; from riding to town in a wagon to owning an automobile. Between 1945 and 1975, the average American family income doubled. My parents considered themselves "middle class." They were proud of their achievements.

However, poor people don't stop being poor just because they have disposable income. Social class is about assumptions and connections and networks, not just about money. That's why I find Charles Taylor's "porous"/"buffered" distinction useful. The distinction goes a long way toward explaining social class.

My parents never became "middle class." Their standard of living went up, but their assumptions never changed. They bought the American Dream, however. Then, in the aftermath of the loss of the Vietnam War, things began to change.

I think one statistic well sums up what happened. Reflect on this: household debt in the US in 1950 was very nearly zero. The property, from farms to houses to cars, belonged for the most part to the people who had possession of it.

Today, household debt in the US is $14 trillion. Much of the property that people in the US "possess" today belongs to banks and credit card companies.

A young couple today born into the circumstances my parents were born into has very little chance of ever even feeling middle class. As a matter of fact, roughly a third of Americans now say they are lower class.

I go into the historical background because, without this incredible outpouring of wealth in the postwar years, people like me—and some of you—would never have moved from a porous understanding to a buffered understanding. My parents lived and died Pentecostal Christians. I'm a humanist. I changed social class. How? The answer is simple: affordable state university education.

The buffered self, Charles Taylor says, has escaped the world of fear. Unlike my parents, I never faced starvation. Or war. Or educational deprivation. Or the feeling of being less-than because of my social location in US society.

As a humanist, I see the luck and happenstance that shuffles the cards of social class as immoral—something to be changed. Quickly.

Blinding and Beheading: One Path, Many Mountains

I have been Don Quixote, always creating a world of my own.

—ANAIS NIN

Science consists of what is the same for everyone, everywhere. Gravity, for example: call it what you will; describe it's origin by means of gods or fairies—still, its results are the same and describable everywhere for everyone. Science: oxygen and its effects—the same everywhere, as Joseph Priestly surmised. Believe in it. Don't believe in it. Yet its effects are the same.

That's science. It's the same for everyone everywhere. All the time. Gravity. Oxygen. The functions of consciousness and the brain. All these are the same everywhere—in different parts of the planet, in different human beings, on Mars.

Religion, however... that's different in different places. It's not the same. The human mind is describable by science. The why of religion will most likely eventually described by science, even though there are at present competing theories. When science discovers the why, the why will be physical.

The what, however, is the product of local forces—customs, flora and fauna, economies, governments. That sort of thing.

The part of religion that will one day most likely be described by science is its physicality. Just now, "mindfulness" is everywhere in popular US culture. Mindfulness is generally understood as the diamond pulled out of its setting in Buddhism. We pull out that diamond by putting "secular" in front of "Buddhism."

The term "secular" can be put in front of any proper noun of a religious variety: secular Hinduism, secular Islam, secular... you get the idea. "Secular" denatures and denudes the term after it; takes away those contingent things such as customs, flora and fauna, economies and governments. It's the difference between going to a temple and reading about a religion in a world religions class.

Often "secular" denotes a way of going back in time to the pure essence of a religion. "Secular Christianity" posits a Jesus who is an existentialist philosopher for all time. Actually, that construction of Jesus merely reflects the values of our time. "Secular Buddhism" posits a Buddha teaching mindfulness.

"Secular" goes a good way toward making religions rational. That's why the term "secular humanism" has been around for a long time. Treating your neighbor as yourself or turning the other cheek have demonstrably positive outcomes, as does sitting down and shutting up. They make rational sense.

I suppose secularity is a logical product of the global village, as cultures collide and blend. Secular's opposite, fundamentalism, is also a product of this collision. The Internet is the Silk Road on steroids.

Just as the shrinking world of the nineteenth century led to the "one mountain, many paths" idea of religions, the global shrinkage of the twenty-first century appears to be shearing religions of their local fleece to . . . spin that fleece into one large blanket of gold.

Now we see that it was one path—human nature—and many mountains, those cultural differences we saw as so important but, upon reflection, are so much window dressing. Important. Defining. But imagined differences, not scientific ones.

Anais Nin realized that she was Don Quixote creating a world of her own. This is the function of any fiction, be it romantic novels or scriptures. Our fictions come from one source: the amazing and fruitful human mind. Our perceptions of our group's specialness in thought, word, or deed at best blinds and at worst . . . beheads. As we celebrate the rich diversity of our world, we do well to remember that a touch of imagination makes the whole world one.

Greenery without People:
The Future of Post-Religious Community

> I don't get it about the natural world.
> Like, greenery,
> without people in it, is supposed
> to do what?
>
> —CHARLES SMITH

How to do religious community in a post-religious world . . . As a senior minister in an urban congregation, it's something I think about every day.

For most urban North Americans, the choice of (non)religious community is as profuse as the choice of breakfast cereals, frozen pizzas, or any other consumer good. We can even find pizza and religious community online.

Despite our interconnecting electronic webs, however, we human beings are still very much tribal animals. There is national allegiance; political affiliation; sports teams; race; religion; which generation you are; which popular or unpopular singer you listen to; which Beatle you like, or whether you've heard of the Beatles; choice in attire; which computer company you buy from . . . an endless list of genetics, geography, time, choices, and fate. Besides all that, there are many—if not most—who do not have any of those choices, which in most cases is not a choice.

Then there is the non-urban. "Where do you go to church?" is still a definitive question in much of rural North America. The answer to that question defines where a person is on the social scale, and even whether someone figures into social calculations beyond the category of "outcast" at all.

It's complicated.

The choices I look to and attempt to nourish are explicitly urban and post-religious. I meet fewer and fewer people who have been damaged by religion in childhood. Fewer and fewer people who feel any compunction to sign on to any religious tradition. Fewer and fewer people who find much beyond historical interest in older interpretive systems.

One advantage I have is that my congregation, First Unitarian Society of Minneapolis, declared itself explicitly humanist and post-religious a century ago. When questions about how to do prayer or child namings or weddings or funerals come up, I can point to a long a rich and history of secular ceremonies. That's because the congregation has remained "religious" in its humanism, meaning that we celebrate life passages communally and still have Sunday morning services, which we have long called "assemblies." In this "religious" orientation we are much like Ethical Culture Societies and the newer phenomenon of Sunday Assemblies.

Will these post-religious congregations survive? That's still an open question. Which is why, looking at the empty rooms in the building during the week, I think of alternative ways of filling them. Small atheist groups. Secular humanist groups. Secular Twelve-Step programs. Advocacy non-profits of various types that align with the mission of the congregation.

My suspicion is that the "butts in pews" measure of congregational success is fast approaching its end. Saving that model is not the point, any more than saving a building has a point other than as a place for people to gather into a tribe dedicated to purposes other than consumerism and identity politics.

The question I ask myself is: What is it we offer the world? My answer is: a post-religious, post-Eurocentric, post-colonial ethics that provides meaning and purpose to individuals, humanity, and the world we live in. The poet Charles Smith says,

> I don't get it about the natural world.
> Like, greenery,
> without people in it, is supposed
> to do what?

People. Gathering in support of each other. People thinking about the way we do things and what we do. That's what matters.

A building without people in it is supposed to do, like, what?

The Transient, the Permanent, and the Stitching Horse: Heresy and Razors

When I was a kid, I loved wandering in the barn on my grandfather's farm. The barn had been built around a two-story log house. In the loft of the barn was a jumble of old farming equipment. My favorite piece of equipment there was what was known as a stitching horse. This was a bench used for harness repair.

A stitching horse consisted of a wooden bench with a pair of wooden arms about two feet long. By stepping on a pedal under the bench, one could squeeze and release the wooden arms. This served as an extra pair of hands when fixing the leather harness for horse farming.

What amazed me most about the stitching horse was how old it must have been, yet it was still in working order. The stitching horse had only one problem, one reason for being in the loft of a barn rather than in a workshop: on our farm, the stitching horse had outlived its usefulness. We were farming with tractors. Everything was made of steel. (Stitching horses are still used for leather working, BTW.)

My grandfather's ingenious stitching horse still worked perfectly well. But it was an excellent answer to a question that wasn't being asked anymore on our farm.

In the early 1840s, just when transcendentalism was stealing the younger generation from Unitarian churches, Unitarian minister Theodore Parker wrote a sermon he called "Discourse on the Transient and Permanent in Religion."

Parker claimed that religious thinking changes over time. Scripture—the Bible—for example, was to Parker a transient means of delivering the truth and had for the most part outlived its usefulness. All the accretions—the miracles and miraculous stories—were antique and needed to be consigned to the loft.

The permanent, Parker argued, consisted of the ethical ideas in scripture that could lead each person toward a deeper understanding of meaning and purpose. (In this, Parker was much like Thomas Jefferson, who took a razor to the Christian scriptures to make a text that was not offensive to basic good sense.)

Parker's ideas were heresy to the old White guys who made up his ministerial fellows. And a breath of fresh air to the upstart transcendentalists.

One hundred seventy-five years later, Parker's is still a heretical proposition. In most Unitarian Universalist congregations, other scriptures have been added to the Christian ones—Hindu, Buddhist, Muslim, and what-have-you—but the old contention remains: that the traditions—scriptures and religions—of the past contain truth and therefore must be studied and respected.

Isn't this view saying, "Yes, we may have implements made of steel, but you have to use that stitching horse when you work on them"?

What is permanent is the human condition. Not the religions that human beings have invented to cope with the human condition. The situation remains the same: the seeds must go into the ground before we can have a harvest. The means of sowing those seeds, however, keeps changing.

Time has shown that Parker was correct, and even more correct than he knew: more and more of religious traditions show their transience with time. The once ubiquitous stitching horse is now an antique or a specialty device.

What's transient and what's permanent?

Truth appears in all human religions in the same way that utility resides in all human tools—that's what they're designed to do. Religions grapple with the truth of the human condition. Yet the only truth that religions communicate are truths of the human heart. Truths concerning meaning and purpose and right action.

What are the truths of religions? What's permanent? You. Your essence. Your human essence.

Is that enough?

Well . . . it has to be. Because that's all we get.

What's in the Way Is the Way: Stoicism and the Spaces Between

> I sit at the roadside;
> The driver changes the wheel.
> I don't like where I'm coming from.
> I don't like where I'm going.
> Why do I watch this wheel change
> Impatiently?

This poem, by German playwright and poet Bertolt Brecht, catches that feeling of being in-between. In process. In liminal space.

We all know about sitting idly by, watching.

The poem reflects a flash of insight. An epiphany. Dissatisfied with where he's been, dissatisfied with where he's going, the speaker in the poem suddenly realizes the absurdity of his impatience to get to a place he doesn't want to go. The poem mentions changing a wheel, not a tire, which is a bit odd. The German word for "wheel" is *rad*, as in "radius." Brecht uses this word, not the word for "tire," *reifen*. I suspect that's because he has *glücksrad* in mind, "wheel of fortune," that fatalistic medieval notion that when you're up you're up and when you're down you're down, and the wheel just keeps on turning.

Why do we sit impatiently, eager to get where we don't want to go? Habit, for one.

Habit means you don't have to think about it. Thinking outside of the box, or off the road you're on, is difficult work. It's easier not to think about it. It's easier just to go to the place you're already headed, even if you know you don't like it all that much. Or at all. It's the street of least resistance.

The chances that we will change a habit once we have started it is one in ten. One in ten. As the poet John Dryden said, "First we make our habits, and then our habits make us."

> Why do I watch this wheel change
> Impatiently?

Where Does Humanism Come From?

The Roman Emperor and Stoic philosopher Marcus Aurelius often found himself on the roadside watching a wheel getting changed. He knew the impatience to be where he didn't want to go.

Stoicism teaches that this liminal space offers the opportunity for decision. Marcus Aurelius said, "What stands in the way becomes the way."

Stoics begin with the assumption that there are roadblocks. That's how things are.

Stoics advise to take a good look at the impediment. If it can't be removed, learn to live with it. If it can, then move it. The Stoic philosopher Epictetus advised, "For heaven's sake, practice being yourself in the small things, then work up to the large."

Epictetus also offered some advice for that impatient person by the roadside in the Brecht poem: "First tell yourself what you want to be, then do what you need to do."

Stoicism has no time for a statement such as, "I'm not the kind of person who . . ." You can't change the fact that wheels need changed. You can change the kind of person you are.

Here's the thing: we're all always sitting by that roadside that Brecht describes. We do or don't like where we have been. We do or don't like where we are going.

What matters is the choice we make in that moment as we watch the changing of the wheel. We can choose to go on to somewhere we don't wish to go.

Or, we can choose something new. Different. Non-habitual. Uncharacteristic. We can choose habit. Or we can choose possibility. As the Stoic emperor put it, "It is not death we should fear, but never beginning to live."

4

The Varieties of Humanism

Community can be defined simply as a group in which free conversation can take place.

—ROLLO MAY

Religious Humanism: What Was Old Is New Again

The Barna Group, a research organization that keeps up with trends in religion, estimates that 48 percent of millennials (those born 1984–2002) are "post-Christian." 48 percent. "Post-Christian" means that they have heard of Christianity, know its claims, swim in its assumptions, and have little to no interest in it as a method for providing meaning and purpose in their lives.

The study point out, "if unchurched Americans were a nation, they would be the eighth largest nation on Earth." The study also shows that statistics indicating "church growth" are church transfers. There are few new conversions.

35 percent of Boomers, 40 percent of Busters, and 48 percent of millennials are unchurched, and many of them have no interest in searching for a church.[1]

Until the mid-twentieth century, what congregation you belonged to was a defining social marker, leading to a great deal of socially induced piety. In much of the United States—especially in urban centers—this is no longer the case.

However, while churches and synagogues no longer meet the needs of roughly half of Americans, the human need for community has, if anything, gotten stronger. This is where the tradition of congregational humanism comes in.

What is nowadays called "religious humanism" developed in two distinct locations: in Ethical Culture societies and in Unitarian and Universalist congregations.

The religious humanism practiced by the Ethical Culture movement was envisioned by Felix Adler, a man who studied to be a rabbi, then became a humanist. Religious humanism as developed by Universalists and Unitarians such as John Dietrich was Protestant in nature.

John Dietrich developed his concept of humanism when he served as the minister at First Unitarian Society of Minneapolis—the congregation I serve.

1. Barna Group, https://www.barna.com/churchless.

It is important to note that neither Felix Adler nor John Dietrich were in-your-face atheists. Felix Adler believed that the god concept would slowly disappear as more and more people found no need for it. Dietrich sought to reinterpret the concept into a descriptor for the natural processes of the universe. There was nothing supernatural in the concept for either man.

What both were clear on is that "god" does not appear to have ever intervened in human history—what is best described as a deist or naturalist position.

Both men saw religions as older interpretive traditions that were based in specific geographic and cultural locations. Both men saw humanism as a universalizing of "truth."

Religious humanism, then, is not—as is often supposed—of necessity "godless." It is based rather in the idea that we don't know what god is up to—if anything—and that we are pretty well on our own in figuring out how to live in the world.

Both men saw congregational life—community—as important, hence the "religious" in "religious humanism." (It should be noted that the term "secular humanism" developed later, in the 1970s.)

Also, I suspect that "religious" may have overstayed its welcome as a descriptor and that "congregational humanism" is a considerably better term going forward.

Felix Adler was a more systematic thinker than John Dietrich. Adler was an academic philosopher; Dietrich's element was the weekly struggle to write a sermon that dealt with the current headlines and questions of ethics that occur in the general mess of daily human life.

Both men believed that humanism, shorn as it was of the ceremonies and terminologies of various religions, could serve to unite humanity across cultural divides. Ethical movements with the characteristics of humanism have, after all, developed across time and cultures, from the Hindu Charvaka movement, an atheist ethical movement from around 600 BCE, to Daoism and Confucianism from around 400 BCE, to Ubuntu, a humanist movement in Africa.

Both men noted the similarity of a "golden rule" across cultures. Adler summarized his key to ethical behavior as: "Act so as to elicit the best in others and thereby in thyself."

One of the major changes in humanism from the time of the founders to our own time is the developing post-Christian and secular Jewish majority.

For Adler and Dietrich, humanism needed to offer a clear alternative to religion. As we know, however, ideas that oppose other ideas often come to resemble what they oppose. In fighting religious dogmas, humanism became dogmatic. Attacks on religious claims, attacks on scriptures, claims and counterclaims became part of humanist practice. This is old fashioned now, at best.

But that was then . . .

The wholesale abandonment of organized religions by millennials does not mean that the generation has abandoned social commitments. Far from it. As many as seven in ten consider themselves social activists. Not merely socially aware—social activists. They are a generation that puts their values into action.

The communities that will be successful—whether they be book clubs, coffee klatches, or congregations—will provide opportunities for collective and meaningful social action.

Religious humanism is the child of another era. Its child, congregational humanism, has a whole new world to dwell in. A world in which religions are interesting antiques and we humans can finally get around to exploring ways to make life better . . . here and now.

Humanism:
A Way Forward

Humanism today is not your grandparents' humanism. The "onward and upward forever" sentiment that permeated liberal Protestantism in the late-nineteenth- and early-twentieth-century United States crumbled as the war of attrition in Vietnam dragged on. That debacle led to the end of the liberal consensus and the so-called culture wars between liberal and conservative worldviews. As the farthest left in religious thinking, humanism was battered and demonized in the popular media.

Decreasing opportunities for education in the US and the pressure to acquire specific skills rather than a broadly liberal education in higher education led to a decrease of interest in the arts, a cornerstone of religious, congregational humanism.

In the wake of what is known as the "linguistic turn" in academic philosophy, language and the scientific method itself began to appear to be unstable foundations for reason. The popularity of deconstruction and post-structuralism in the academy sounded to non-specialists like an invitation to relativism and a repudiation of reason and the scientific method.

This appeared to many people as justification for superstitions and an unexamined life as methods for escaping what appeared to moral relativism.

What did "free thinking" mean in such a new world? Weren't we all merely products of our time and place? And what of the much-touted individualism?

Humanism has often been accused of an over-reliance on reason. This was the case. From the first blush of the Enlightenment until the ashes of the Second World War and after, Reason was for many in the Western World another idol set up in the place of the gods that the Enlightenment had shattered.

Firstly, ask: Which group did more for the benefit of humanity—the group that made an idol of Reason, or the group that continued the worship of the gods of monotheism?

Secondly, since many humanists have a greater commitment to the truth than to reason, post-WWII thinking has demolished the sacredness of reason. For example, *Philosophy in the Flesh*, a 1999 book by George Lakoff and Mark Johnson, begins like this:

> The mind is inherently embodied.
> Thought is mostly unconscious.
> Abstract concepts are largely metaphorical.

Yes, for those of us committed to following truth wherever it leads, contemporary anthropology and neuroscience have dealt a one-two punch to the concept of "pure reason." We know that.

The three sentences above deal a far more devastating blow to conventional concepts of divinity than of reason, however. After all, these concepts have been arrived at through the use of reason (and intuition) and reason's method, which is experiment, and they contribute to the project of reason itself: understanding things in the most useful manner possible and the one that most closely comports with the facts as we know them.

What's "heady" about reason? Well, it's true that the "god" that Westerners made of reason—reason with a capital R—could be transcendent, disembodied, above it all, just as was the European concept of god at the time.

Both ideas are not only wrong, they are dangerous.

Humanists have gotten over it. With the work of John Dewey, for example, who died in 1952. Dewey's pragmatist method told us that truth is contingent. That "truth" is not about transcendent, eternal ways of things but rather about what works.

Far from "heady," reason is about getting the hands dirty by actually touching the world's body.

Spiritual but Not . . . Keep Talking

Literary critic Terry Eagleton said, "The din of conversation is as much meaning as we shall ever have." I like that. On first glance, it appears to be bleak—human conversation is all the meaning there is?

But imagine what human conversation has given us. Imagine the din of conversation under the porches and under the trees in Athens during the time of Socrates. Imagine the din of conversation in Baghdad in the late 700s when an institution called the House of Wisdom opened its doors—an attempt to gather all the wisdom in the world. Think of the din of conversation in Florence that led to the Renaissance. The din of conversation in Shakespeare's London. The din of conversation in cafes that created the Vienna Circle at the beginning of the twentieth century. The din of conversation in the Paris of the 1920s. Or Greenwich Village. Or North Beach in San Francisco in the 1950s, which gave rise to the Beat Generation. Think of the din of conversation in Liverpool, England that led to the Beatles. Or the din of conversation in a little recording studio called Sub Pop, which led to the "Seattle sound," better known as grunge.

Too often we think of lonely geniuses, but genius is seldom lonely. Shakespeare and his Globe Theatre was not the only show in town. Shakespeare's London had twenty-seven public theatre venues. More than fifty British bands made up the so-called British invasion. The Beatles weren't alone.

Looked at from this perspective—from the view of what gets created in the crucible of human sharing—Eagleton's phrase does not sound quite so bleak: "The din of conversation is as much meaning as we shall ever have." Why ever would we want more than human conversation?

Would we want a voice from on high coming to proclaim the once and final truth? Isn't the mystery more beautiful—the stabs in the dark of the millions of human beings who have taken part in this great din of conversation, this lovely human project of creating meaning?

I believe in community. A place where people talk with each other. In coffee houses. In bars. In streets and market squares—public spaces and the din of conversation—this is the meaning of meaning. And it is why totalitarian regimes fear the public square and religions burn books.

The term "conversation" originally meant intimacy with others. It also meant sexual intercourse. Only later did the term take on its present meaning of talking.

Let's just say there's something intimate about conversation.

What if the increasing din of human conversation, and perhaps its increasing complexity, is the hope of humankind? Would it be so bad if the talking that led to the Renaissance and a band called Nirvana is all the heaven we humans shall ever know?

Let's take one conversation as an example. Two human beings, Michael Murphy (not the pop singer) and Frederic Spiegelberg, started a conversation. They agreed that the human spiritual impulse need not necessarily follow any one religious tradition. They thought that people could be "spiritual but not religious." That phrase is a cliché now, a whipping boy for various dogmas. But in its day the phrase was a radical new thought. Spiegelberg published a book titled *The Religion of No Religion*.

The two men founded an institution called the Esalen Institute. Whatever you may think of what the Esalen Institute became, look at how pervasive a conversation between two people back in the 1950s has become. "Spiritual but not religious" as a concept is destroying traditional religions in the United States. And Murphy and Spiegelberg would not be upset by that. The Esalen motto is "No one captures the flag." No religion has all the truth. And science doesn't either.

Aren't gratitude and grace and compassion and love and astonishment part of human nature? Part of our evolution? How could any one religion steal the flag of wonder or awe? As a matter of fact, how do any of these things have anything at all to do with religion?

Isn't gratitude and grace and compassion and love and astonishment just as available in art, in music, in poetry? Available to each of us somewhere in the din of conversation?

Isn't science a conversation too?

Pragmatic philosopher John Dewey once said, "Growth itself is the *only moral end*." To philosophers a word like "only" means a lot more than it does to most of us. And here, in the twenty-first century, looking back on the wreckage and horror of the twentieth, it's easy to dismiss such a sentiment with a "meh" and move on to the next sound bite. And "self-help"? Fahgettaboudit!

After all, we've had it up to our ears with "growth," haven't we? Now we know something Dewey did not: that when "personal" met "growth," sparks flew and wedding bells rang, and out of that union many fortunes and many suckers have been born. It's easy at this point to cynically dismiss the whole enchilada.

"Development" is an even more problematic word. "Personal development." Ugh. What is the "personal." And in the communal sphere, some of us live in the "developed world," where we have "developers" producing something called . . . "developments." These developments have produced a great deal of sterile, ugly space.

Somewhere, sometime in the last century, many came to believe that the "onward and upward" march of humanity wasn't such a sound formula for growth. Somewhere back there "onward" and "upward" and "developed" too often began to mean treading on the heads of the poor, over the bodies of animals and plants, across the last bits of pristine Earth.

Somewhere in there humanists such as Dewey, who thought that it was all up to humanity itself, not a supernatural being, to do the growing and developing, began to be dismissed as naive. Somewhere in there the neo-orthodox, such as theologian Karl Barth, began to say, "Can't you see that Satan, or at the least humanity's flawed nature, is in charge and must be handled with a chain?"

When Dewey said "growth itself is the only moral end," he meant us; he meant growing, developing, cultivating the human psyche and human interactions, not the wetlands or the aquifers. He meant our individual and communal selves. Dewey meant development and growth in such things as ethics and art and democracy, not in the grossness of the national product. Or the boundaries of empire.

In this, Dewey was joining a long line of non-Christian Western philosophers who taught that *eudaimonia*, "human flourishing," arises through an "examined life" lived in pursuit of virtue. It isn't about human perfection, but rather about being a bit better than we were born, a bit better than other primates such as us.

The human right to this pursuit may have been what Thomas Jefferson was talking about when he wrote that human beings have three "unalienable rights," one of which is the "pursuit of happiness."

That this curious and intriguing phrase gets discussed far less in the United States than what the Second Amendment means, and what it allows, perhaps tells us more than we want to know about the development of the

US since Jefferson wrote the Declaration of Independence. I suspect that Jefferson would have agreed with Dewey that democracy itself "begins in conversation." That's the communal aspect of growth.

As another fan of the pursuit of virtue, Scottish philosopher Alasdair MacIntyre, put it, "I believe the process of understanding the problems is itself a good." This is not about talk; it is about conversation—and you can't converse alone. Conversation is democracy. It is communal. And it is growth when we converse rather than pontificate—an ability based in individual growth.

If the pursuit of happiness were defined as the ability to pursue questions of virtue, isn't it interesting to consider what it would mean for each US citizen to have the right to pursue happiness?

The pursuit of happiness . . . Should I head for the self-help section of my local bookstore to begin my pursuit? Uh, no. The pursuit of happiness—the pursuit of virtue, truth, meaning, and democracy—exists as conversation for a good reason: it's communal as well as personal. Perhaps that's the biggest reason Jefferson's line gets ignored—we have defined happiness as an individual pursuit in the United States, land of individualists and of self-help. That solipsism has had its logical outcome in mass murder and misery.

The personal growth Dewey advocated was a personal growth within the larger communal whole. The pursuit of virtue, after all, is about how we treat others far more than it is about how we treat ourselves. Dewey had in mind the ideal of Socratic dialogue, which isn't easy to live up to. It can't be found on TV. Or among pundits.

Growth itself is the only moral end because it is about striving to be a better human being for the good of the whole, for human flourishing. The gods can't be much help with that. It is a profoundly human-ist thing to do.

Yes, the din of your conversation is as much meaning as we shall ever have—but it is enough.

Keep talking. Increase the din. Converse. Remake the human reality.

Congregational Humanist Liturgy: Creating a Religion-Neutral Zone

The Daoist philosopher Zhuangzi (370–287 BCE) told this story:

>Once three friends were discussing life. One said:
>"Can people live together and know nothing of life,
>work together and produce nothing?
>Can people fly around in the air
>and forget to exist,
>forever and ever?"
>
>The three friends looked at each other and burst out laughing.
>
>They had no explanation, and so
>they were better friends than before.
>
>Then one of the friends died.
>
>Upon hearing of the death, Confucius sent a disciple
>to help the two remaining friends
>chant the funeral obsequies.
>
>Upon arrival, the Confucian found that one of the friends had composed a song,
>and the other was playing upon a lute.
>
>The two friends sang:
>
>"Hey, Sung Hu, where'd you go?
>Hey, Sung Hu, where'd you go?
>You have gone where you really were all along,

The Varieties of Humanism

And we are here, damn it, we are here!"

When the Confucian heard this
he burst into the room and said,

"May I inquire where you found this
in all the books of funeral obsequies,
this silly singing in the presence
of the dearly departed?"

The two friends looked at each other, laughed, and said:

"Poor fellow! He doesn't know the new liturgy!"[1]

Ideally, a humanist congregational gathering is a religion-neutral zone. When I say "religion-neutral," I'm not being ironic or clever. A humanist liturgy is not an anti-religion zone or a no-religion zone. It is a place without sectarianism. The thought of such a liturgy may be, like the new liturgy for the dead friend in Zhuangzi's story, shocking to the orthodox. But it is shocking only in concept. In execution, it is, again as Zhuangzi relates, fresh and heartfelt. The congregation may feel like the three friends:

They had no explanation, and so
they were better friends than before.

New liturgy and fresh thinking avoids clichés. The Confucian (so to speak) in the room may want to hear the old words—words such as "prayer," "hymn," "god," "soul"—but there's a reason "obsequies" easily become obsequious. That reason has to do with mind-forged manacles.

Why ask the Muslims, Hindus, Earth-centered practitioners, atheists, Skeptics, Cynics, Stoics, et cetera in the room (and why shouldn't they be in the room?) to listen to the language of their would-be or some-time oppressors? Sure, those for whom Christian liturgical language makes sense will be baffled, asking, "May I inquire where you found this in all the books?"

Humanists will have a chuckle. Our liturgy arises from the old questions asked in new ways—ways we hope lead to lives of deeper meaning and authenticity. (Authenticity is, I think, the point of Zhungzi's story.) Isn't the question at every funeral,

---

1. Adapted from a translation by Thomas Merton, in Merton, *Way of Chuang Tzu*.

After the Bloody Mary Game

> Hey, Sung Hu, where'd you go?
> Hey, Sung Hu, where'd you go?

And isn't the deepest emotion at every funeral this one?:

> And we are here, damn it, we are here!

Religion-neutral isn't religion-free. (Nor is it anti-Christian merely because there's nothing of Christianity in it.) It's a space where, in the face of the oldest questions, we sing a new song, a song of inclusion and freedom.

The "Trinsics":
Where Are You Comin' From?

Psychologist Gordon Allport argued that there are two types of religious experience: the extrinsic and the intrinsic. Extrinsic religious orientation has little to do with religion and lots to do with social norms, rules, and regulations. Allport said extrinsic orientation functions "to provide security and solace, sociability and distraction, status and self-justification." This sort of religion is a means to an end. (Sound familiar?)

Intrinsic religious orientation, on the other hand, is the end in itself. For those oriented toward intrinsic religion, their religion becomes their meaning and purpose in life. The means *is* the end. The religious commitment shapes the life.

This is as far as Allport took the idea, but Daniel Batson, who holds doctorates in both psychology and theology, posited a third religious orientation, what he called "quest." Watson says,

> An individual who approaches religion in this way recognizes that he or she does not know, and probably never will know, the final truth about such matters. Still the questions are deemed important, and however tentative and subject to changes, answers are sought.

This sounds an awful lot like Unitarian Universalism. Realizing that the answers—all the answers—are time bound, socially bound, class bound, and tentative is a wise way of looking at the old answers to the old problems and the new answers to those old problems. Wisdom.

As I see it, wisdom, when it comes to religious and philosophical questions, is about being two things: humble and realistic. This wisdom centers around an old Daoist and Epicurean and Stoic insight: we must accept the nature of reality itself—and the reality of nature—or we can't be content and have our eyes open at the same time.

That's the essence, isn't it: the goal is to both have our eyes open and be as content as we can at the same time.

There are ways to be content—even happy—and *not* look at what is real—staying drunk or stoned all the time, for example. Or staying depressed or optimistic all the time. Or retail therapy. All those are lies we tell ourselves.

If the quest is authenticity, life is about both gaining and losing. To pretend that life is not about loss is a fool's game.

Religious maturity is about realism, and realism requires humility in the face of life's challenges. Furthermore, as Batson pointed out, it's about accepting the fact that the search is all we have—that the search itself is the challenge and the answer.

Arriving at "truth" merely means you've given up the search. Science is open-ended; philosophy is open-ended; all the fine arts are open-ended—this is what creativity is, when every new thing is new. As in art and science and philosophy, stopping the search in religious thinking means you've given up any hope of renewal, or creativity.

Religious thinking—thinking about the ultimate meaning and purpose of human life on this planet—must both involve the chance to continuously evolve with time and offer some hope for the human condition—our condition—itself.

To have any validity beyond mere fantasy, religious thinking must be oriented toward greater human flourishing—greater flourishing that human beings have yet achieved.

As the Daoists and the Buddhists and the Epicureans and the Stoics and many others all realized, each day is new and different, with new challenges for each of us. What do we need each day? I'd say three things: equanimity, compassion, and wisdom.

Equanimity is about taking what comes and dealing with the challenges. Compassion is about remembering that each person we meet is just like us, with the same capacity for fear, hope, and dreams. Wisdom helps us find equanimity and compassion. Wisdom takes all our knowledge and experience and boils it down, focuses it so that we can face life with equanimity and compassion.

No, we don't want our moral aspirations to remain shadowy and vague. We want our daily practices become more than navel-gazing: we want and need our inner work to be preparation for outer action.

Then, we have realized and owned our agency—realized the fact that what we do in the world matters . . . for both good and ill. And we begin to tilt that scale more toward the good than the ill. Then you're coming from somewhere.

The Proof's in the Pudding
(or What's Churchy about Church?)

I'm sometimes asked how humanists can have "church" without invoking god. Here's how I think about it. Imagine this scenario: when Imhotep in ancient Egypt invoked the great god Ra, he was (actually) invoking the human consciousness, not Ra Almighty.

Imagine this: when Zadok, son of Ahitub, entered the holy of holies of Solomon's brand new temple, perhaps he was talking to the greatest power on this Earth—the human imagination.

Imagine this: when the evangelist Billy Graham made his vast alter calls in stadiums across North America, the Christ that thousands flocked to was . . . the human psyche.

Whatever you think about powers beyond, imagine this for just a moment. Entertain the thought for just a moment that every shaman, priest, and prophet who has ever lived . . . has created worship without god because . . . there never has been six or three or one to begin with.

But wait! Isn't there more to the question? Because, even granted the accuracy of my imaginings, didn't Imhotep and Zadok and Billy Graham each have the advantage of speaking to people who shared a subjective reality?

Didn't the Egyptians of Imhotep's time have a mental image of Ra and the Hebrews of Zadok's time have a notion of Yahweh and the Christians of Billy Graham's time a common picture of Christ the Lord?

Good question . . .

Did they, really? Are people like that? Or did the priests and preachers have, rather, the apparatus of worship embedded in a particular place and time—Ra's temple, Yahweh's temple, or the vast football stadiums of Jesus with great PA systems?

Can we seriously argue that each ancient Egyptian had an identical psychological understanding of Ra? Not likely. But they did have a temple, didn't they? Doesn't the very fact of the rabbinic tradition argue that Hebrew worshipers exited Zadok's services with very different views of ultimate reality? Still, they had that temple, didn't they?

Weren't there as many Christs as there were Christians in Billy Graham's vast alter calls? Yet they came to that structure of power and fame called a stadium or an auditorium, didn't they? They came to hear Billy.

Could it be that what they all had in common is an apparatus for worship that individual psyches journeyed to?

What's so churchy about church? The apparatuses of worship change with time, as do the words and the concepts. It is the human mind and human needs for purpose and meaning that remain the same and come to the temple, the stadium, or the storefront church. These are what remain the same.

For humanists, that's as holy as it gets. And that's fine: the proof is in the pudding. Ra's pudding doesn't do much for many of us. But the pudding of gathering together into community is quite tasty.

Just imagine that the point of worship (humanists prefer "assembly") is calling individuals into community. Imagine that a community created in this way agrees to agree—despite individual understandings—on particular values that sometimes—in the best-case scenario—lead to objective common actions that may be considered moral and ethical (actions more focused and effective because they spring from a common purpose).

That's what "worship"—uh, assembling—will or won't do. Gathering to invoke Ra or any of the deities (or no deity at all) leads to the same thing—the human mind imbued with meaning and purpose and communal actions that matter.

Imagine . . .

Nature, Nurture, Murder:
The Lesson of Eugenics

In the world of superheroes, it's called an "origin story"—that trauma that led to the superhero being, uh, super. Poor little Bruce Wayne watches helplessly as his parents are murdered. Superman rockets off the planet Krypton, sent away by his father moments before the planet explodes, only to find himself in Kansas where a loving couple adopts him and imbues him with truth, justice, and the American Way.

Magneto and Professor X start out as just normal . . . mutants . . . but life experience sends one on to found the good-guy X-Men and the other to . . . electrical evil.

Clearly, the creators of superheroes believe that nurture trumps nature in that long debate between nature and nurture. But the more we know about genetics, the more we have to ask, is that true? Do our genes make us do it, whatever the "it" might be?

Science has been known to give us answers that we are not culturally capable of understanding. The most egregious moment of that in the twentieth century was the eugenics movement; that is, the belief that "better babies" could be produced by selective human breeding, and the corollary belief that those born with disabilities and those of races not of Western European origin were inferior.

It was part and parcel of the early birth control movement. Liberal preachers preached it. Liberal people practiced it. And it led ultimately to the atrocities of Nazi Germany.

It also led, in the US, to immigration laws barring most people not of Western European origin and the forced sterilization of thousands of people. Proponents believed they could eradicate mental disorders through eugenics. They believed they could eradicate alcoholism.

Forced sterilization for those in mental institutions was a practice upheld by the US Supreme Court. Thousands of poor people were forcibly sterilized. And the practice of requiring sterilization as a precondition for receiving welfare checks continued in some states into the 1970s.

Their motto was, "Eugenics is the self-direction of evolution."

Fact is, the Nazis got many of their ideas from the United States and used the example of the US to justify their actions to other nations all through the 1930s.

Today, we know this behavior well as the rhetoric of neo-Nazis, the Ku Klux Klan, and some far-out right-wing politicians. But liberals?

I don't want in any way to justify these beliefs. They are despicable. Yet dismissing these ideas as something from the dark past is a very bad idea. Rather, we should look to that terrible chapter of American history as a cautionary tale. Because, besides being based in the most virulent forms of racism and ableism, political progressives also saw eugenics as good science—the latest in scientific knowledge. That's the cautionary tale: eugenics appealed to the very people most open to the theory of natural selection.

Why? One reason is that they applied the idea of natural selection—still not well understood by most people in the early twentieth century—to an idea most Americans knew very well at the time—the selective breeding of animals. Remember the motto I mentioned: "Eugenics is the self-direction of evolution." Nowadays most people who look at the matter know that natural selection can't be self-selected—the time frame is way too long for human beings to affect, or even comprehend, for that matter. But most people did not know that at the time.

Here's how the fatal error occurred: We have cats and dogs and ridable horses because of selective breeding. People figured this out a loooong time ago. My grandparents, who could barely read and write, were experts at selective breeding. Most farmers were.

People knew that traits can be affected in a short time among animals, and so they assumed that human genetics could be affected in a short time. And that simply isn't true—not in animals such as human beings that have long lives, anyway. Fruit flies are a different story. As is the famous case of the tube (subway) mice in London that have evolved in about a century and a half to have grey coats that exactly match the color of paint used on the bottom of the London train tunnels. But people aren't fruit flies or mice. Scientific ideas often become dangerous when they are applied to culture or human life on a micro-level.

Remember that Charles Darwin knew almost nothing about genetics: Mandel's work on peas was in existence in Darwin's lifetime, but Darwin never encountered the studies.

Remember that the structure of DNA was not discovered until 1953, well after the horrors of Nazism. The first draft of the human genome appeared in 2001.

To that we must add that the overt racist and ableist assumptions in the US at the time made for the perfect environment for the eugenics movement. Racism and ableism permeated US society—from outright segregationists to progressives to just about everybody. Heck, even the Homeopathy Society supported eugenics.

We see the same sort of misapplication of science today: Despite what New Age gurus might claim, people are not lonely because we live in an expanding universe. We can't walk through walls because there is lots of space between atoms. We don't vibrate with cosmic vibrations because of string theory.

And you don't speed up natural selection through eugenics. The time scales of the two are completely different. All these are the realm of hucksters. And, in the case of eugenics, racists.

Takeaway: when science appears to support your preconceptions and prejudices, watch out!

No, there isn't a superhero who became Spider-Man because he was bitten by an irradiated spider. But here are some things that are real science that we easily forget:

Genetic research has taught us that the entire concept of race is a fiction. A mistake. There are no genetically identifiable races. *Homo sapiens* developed along about 200,000 years ago and some *Homo sapiens* began leaving Africa something along about 80,000 years ago. Human generations are roughly twenty-five years, which means that some *Homo sapiens* left Africa about 3,000 generations ago; other *Homo sapiens*, such as our Somali neighbors, left in this generation. We're all immigrants out of Africa.

Despite what the racists of the early twentieth century believed, there is no "race" in the *Homo sapiens* population, only separation by time and cultural difference.

You may have read that President Obama is related to Harry Truman, Dick Cheney, George Bush, and Brad Pitt. This is not urban legend. But it doesn't prove a whole lot either, except that human beings are all related, and that we tend to notice the famous and infamous ones and not the unfamous ones.

Until everyone understands this, we will have not only the egregious lunatics such as the neo-Nazis and the Ku Klux Klan, but also the casual clichés that still permeate our culture and destroy the lives of too many people.

Poor little Bruce Wayne. He could have been a man of leisure. Superman might have hung out on Krypton (or at least Kansas). And there's no telling what nature might have had Magneto and Professor X doing. As for us, we must continue wondering and speculating just how much of what we do is up to us and how much is up to our stars . . . and our genes. All will be well, so long as we remember humility in the face of a very large universe.

Building Better Primates

I sometimes enjoy reading columns by *New York Times* op-ed writer David Brooks. His opinions are not of the usual "conservatives say the darnedest things" variety, and his February 3, 2015 column, "Building Better Secularists," is no exception.

First off, Brooks admits some inconvenient truths that most apologists for religion won't, such as the fact that evidence says secular people are more—not less—"moral" and law-abiding than religious people. (Go figure!) Brooks also faces the fact that "atheist, agnostic, or without religious affiliation" is a fast-growing group, making up one out of five Americans, and one in three of the "youngest Americans."

He might also mention that people in the European Union—the old "Christendom"—now split fifty-fifty over the question of the existence of a god and, furthermore, in most EU countries attendance at houses of worship is in the single digits. (For comparison, one in three Americans attend at least once a month.) In this context, I think it might be more clarifying to call people "post-religious" rather than "secular"—many are done with religion, but it's not about rejection; it's about irrelevance in their lives.

These numbers alone should end debate. But as a leader of a humanist congregation, I am intrigued by the question of how post-religious people can live more meaningful and purposeful lives in community. Brooks suggests that post-religious people face three challenges: build-it-yourself morality, build-it-yourself communities, and build-it-yourself moral motivation. The religious, in Brooks' view, have all these provided ready-made by tradition.

However, isn't it true that part of the consumerist American spirituality industry, from the eighteenth century to the present, has been exactly about build-it-yourself morality, build-it-yourself communities, and build-it-yourself moral motivation—well exemplified by the Church of Latter Day Saints or Scientology?

Strip-mall spirituality and its ability to adjust to both the place and the times is one of the reasons more Americans still attend congregations, but the connection to tradition—despite the claims of the strip-mall churches—is often tenuous at best. I agree with Brooks that this is a problem. That's why I am, in addition to being post-religious, also a humanist—I believe in building community and finding moral direction in a responsible manner, grounded as closely as possible to reality.

I am the senior minister of a congregation that has been humanist for one hundred years (since 1916). That's a bit of time to have developed a humanist tradition of community, morality, and motivation. All without reference to any gods or supernatural woo-woo. It's not all that new, after all, unless you see Claude Monet as the hottest new trend.

How has the congregation done this? Well, tradition for one. Two thousand years ago, when the newbie Christians came around, they suppressed and killed off some very fine and very ancient communities in which morality and moral cultivation had been taken seriously for a very long time. That's one way. We look back past the newbie colonizers. (Oh, and there's also China.)

Beyond that, the religions that now predominate in the world are very young in comparison to the evolved morality of the human brain. Why are the same things taboo in various and sundry religions and philosophies all over the planet? Because human beings evolved morality long before the rise of the Iron Age religions that now dominate the world.

Yes, I agree with David Brooks that a default and consumerist secularity is not good for anyone. I don't, however, agree that we humans have a "spiritual urge" toward "purity, self-transcendence and sanctification." Two of those are marketing terms as far as I can see . . . creating a need to be filled—smart marketing, bad philosophy. From my perspective, human beings are pure and sanctified enough the day we're born.

But I do agree that we can do better. Always better.

Sure, I agree that meaning and purpose are born of those things that transcend individualism. "Self-transcendence" arises when we realize that primates diverged from other mammals eighty-five million years ago . . . and we've still got a long way to go. And that way includes new—post-religious—ways of thinking.

Go, primates!

The Spiritual Practice of Agnosticism

The Aesop fable about the boy who cried wolf has long been viewed as a cautionary tale about lying. The boy knowingly cried "Wolf!" merely to disturb the villagers. The boy eventually paid the price in dead sheep when the villagers stopped responding.

There is another and more dangerous way of crying wolf, however: continually calling "Wolf!" because there might be one but there might not.

In this way of crying wolf, the boy is expressing his fears—his own psychodrama. He may even be utterly convinced that a wolf is threatening and nearby. He may even be imagining what a wolf attack might look like. Still, despite the boy's true alarm, there is no wolf, and the villagers are wasting their time running to help the boy. Wasting time that would be better taken with other ventures.

As an agnostic, I'm very aware that we agnostics are often seen as fence-sitters—the tepid ones choosing neither hot nor cold. Why can't we just buck up and admit that we're atheists? Or why can't we admit that we have a soft spot for one god or another? Why can't we just cry wolf or shut up?

Contrary to the cliché, agnosticism isn't about not deciding. It's about honestly facing what we know about knowing itself. It is, as the Victorian biologist T. H. Huxley—who coined the term—said, "not a creed but a method." (Atheism is a creed because it is a belief, like theism.)

Agnosticism is a method that is, I believe, a spiritual practice like Christian centering prayer or Buddhist meditation.

When Huxley first used the word in print in 1889, he contrasted his confidence in human knowledge with that of the convinced believers. He said,

> They were quite sure they had attained a certain "gnosis"—had, more or less successfully, solved the problem of existence; while I was quite sure I had not, and had a pretty strong conviction that the problem was insoluble.

> So I took thought, and invented what I conceived to be the appropriate title of "agnostic." It came into my head as suggestively antithetic to the "gnostic" of Church history, who professed to know so much about the very things of which I was ignorant.

Gnostic in Greek means "knowledge." In the Western world, we know the term best from the early Christian movement called Gnosticism, which claimed esoteric knowledge of the workings of the universe. Such knowledge, Huxley pointed out, can be neither proven nor disproven. The Gnostics claimed to have "solved the problem of existence." Huxley, however, wasn't so sure of their untestable opinions. (Neither, it might be mentioned, was the church so sure of their solution.)

In other words, Gnosticism wasn't about knowing, it was about belief. Agnosticism is about how and what we know.

Boiled down to its simplest formulation, the way of agnosticism according to Huxley is: "do not pretend conclusions are certain that are not demonstrated or demonstrable."

No matter how convinced you are that the wolf is near, don't cry wolf until you see one.

This is not fence-sitting or vacillation. It is, rather, a commitment to the active search for what we can know. In this way it is much like the spiritual practice of *via negativa*, a method of removing those things that are not god in order to discover god. Huxley, however, saw his method as a positive rather than negative path. He wrote:

> . . . Agnosticism is not properly described as a "negative" creed, nor indeed as a creed of any kind, except in so far as it expresses absolute faith in the validity of a principle, which is as much ethical as intellectual. This principle may be stated in various ways, but they all amount to this: that it is wrong for a man to say he is certain of the objective truth of a proposition unless he can produce evidence which logically justifies that certainty. That is what agnosticism asserts and, in my opinion, is all that is essential to agnosticism.[1]

Huxley made it very clear that scientific materialists don't have the answers either. No one does. All of us find ourselves improvising with as much information as we can scramble together—as have all people for all of human history. Agnostics are committed, however, to the common human project of learning more and more. Of knowing what is actually here, not

---

1. Huxley, "Agnosticism and Christianity."

what we only imagine. This commitment requires us to have active minds engaged in continual searching.

As psychologist Ellen J. Langer puts it in her book *Mindfulness*, "Just as mindlessness is the rigid reliance on old categories, mindfulness means the continual creation of new ones."

The method of agnosticism is a way of being mindful. A way of being in the present moment and making that moment an open and creative matrix. Agnosticism is a commitment to only crying "Wolf!" when such a cry will do actual good.

"God" is a complicated answer to a simple question: Why do I have consciousness in a universe that doesn't appear to give a damn?

The answer to the question is: conditions were such that the type of consciousness you have could develop in a universe such as this one. That's the simple answer. The answer that employs Occam's razor.

The "god" answer exists, first, because the correct answer could not have occurred to most of the ancient peoples considering the question. Second, it exists because of inertia—religions in motion tend to stay in motion. Third, the correct answer, at first blush, does not appear to be satisfying.

Yet, I must ask: To see reality as it is—isn't this the goal of philosophies and religions? Isn't this the call that the human consciousness hears? To see things as they are?

That there is suffering in the world does not imply that the world supplies an answer or anecdote to the suffering. It implies that living things will attempt to avoid suffering. The poet William Blake said, "The cut worm forgives the plow." Does it?

Use Your Words, Earn Your Words

Poets say that a word must be earned. By that we mean that using a word such as—oh, let's say—"plashy" needs to happen in a context that warrants using a word that doesn't tend to occur in regular conversation, unless one is working a crossword puzzle.

"Plashy" means something along the lines of "having lots of puddles," but the average speaker of English says "lots of puddles," not "plashy." Therefore, the wisdom of post-Victorian poets goes: It's bad form to use "plashy" merely because the word sounds poetic and deep. You've got to earn using a word like "plashy" by creating a context in which the word is no longer merely poetic, but just the perfect, inevitable word for the context.

A similar sort of word is "bosky," which means something like "having lots of trees." Notice that I have provided definitions for both words, because even speakers of English as a native tongue often don't know these words. They are, in the quaint language of dictionaries, "poeticisms." A poeticism itself, "poeticism" means, according to *Merriam-Webster*, a "poetic, trite, or strained expression."

Yes, that's the challenge of poetry—using a trite or strained or clichéd word as if it were the only possible word that could be used in that context. That's what it means to a poet to "earn" a word.

Some words are hard-earned.

That's all I ask—as a poet—when someone uses the poeticism "god." Has the use of the word been earned? It needs to be inevitable and the only one that will do in the context. Is it the only word available that isn't poetic or clichéd in the context?

Is it, really? There isn't one just as good? Oh, say, "universe" or "complexity" or "unsolved mystery"?

Think about it. Earn it.

So, off I go into the bosky dell of plashy delight, using only words I've earned.

See you there, in that windswept plain.

Spiritual but Not Superstitious

"Spirituality" is an emotion. Sometimes it is a consciously adopted attitude toward the world we see around us. Sometimes it hits us unexpectedly. A "spiritual experience" can be anything from the gladness of singing a song we love to the inexpressible "mystical" experience of feeling one with all that is.

All great feelings. But not a mystery. Psychologist Daniel Khaneman in his ground-breaking book *Thinking, Fast and Slow* outlines how the head/heart or body/soul distinction actually functions. Fast thinking, which Khaneman calls System One, is our fight-or-flight selves. The visceral reaction. Slow thinking, System Two, is our reason and problem-solving abilities.

As we learn more about these systems, we see more clearly what techniques and technologies best trigger responses. When the rhythm of the music reaches 180 beats per minute, we feel like dancin'.

For my money, the most insightful writer on the subject of spirituality and mysticism is Jiddu Krishnamurti. Born into British-occupied India, young Krishnamurti was taken under the wing of the Theosophists and trained in that mystical tradition. The Theosophists thought Krishnamurti would be the great "World Teacher" that they predicted would come to Earth.

Krishnamurti eventually renounced Theosophy but did indeed become a great teacher, a synthesizer of spiritual and religious thinking from all over the world.

One of Krishnamurti's gifts was a keen BS detector. Therefore, when Krishnamurti talks about spirituality and mysticism, I listen.

His key insight goes like this: "It is only when you listen without the idea, without thought, that you are directly in contact."

Listening without preconception, without judgment, without the interference of ego; listening in order to hear, to experience—right now, with as little of the usual interference as possible. Unmediated experience.

This sort of listening requires presence in the moment. It requires us to be in the place of the breath and that mental space that is at once maximum concentration and maximum letting go. This experience may be achieved by various techniques, from mediation to fasting to merely looking up at the stars.

From Christian centering prayer to Zen Buddhist *zazen* to the various yogas, human beings have developed techniques for getting to this space between. Since these techniques trigger System One—fast thinking—they feel visceral, spiritual.

Woo without the Woo-Woo

"Mysticism" is a technique aimed at achieving a "mystical experience." This experience is a feature of brain function and has little to do with specific religious or philosophical practices, except insofar as many religions aim for the experience and have techniques for achieving it.

Some traditions are overt about it—Sufism, for example, or shamanistic practice, or transcendentalism. Take, for instance, this passage from Henry David Thoreau's *Walden*:

> In any weather, at any hour of the day or night, I have been anxious to improve the nick of time, and notch it on my stick too; to stand on the meeting of two eternities, the past and the future, which is precisely the present moment; to toe that line. (ch. 1)

In 1838, Ralph Waldo Emerson wrote in his journal, "What is there of the divine in a load of bricks? What is there of the divine in a barber's shop or a privy? Much. All." In his poem "Woodnotes II" Emerson says this:

> Onward and on, the eternal Pan
> Who layeth the world's incessant plan,
> Halteth never in one shape,
> But forever doth escape,
> Like wave or flame, into new forms
> Of gem, and air, of plants and worms.
> I, that to-day am a pine,
> Yesterday was a bundle of grass.

Or as Emily Dickinson put it,

> In the name of the Bee—
> And of the Butterfly—
> And of the Breeze—Amen!

A new trinity! A trinity of the natural and observable world available here and now in a New England garden.

The transcendentalists were a threat to the orthodox religion of their day. And, when we look at their ideas closely, they remain a threat.

Traditionally, religions build walls around their various methods of achieving mystical experiences, then hierarchy and priestly clubs pretended special knowledge. Krishnamurti again: "I maintain that Truth is a pathless land, and you cannot approach it by any path whatsoever, by any religion, by any sect."

To the chagrin of priests, mystical experiences are experiences beyond words. They are subjective events. They entail a feeling of boundless, danger-less belonging. A feeling of timelessness. A feeling that everything is OK.

Thoreau again:

> You will pardon some obscurities, for there are more secrets to my trade than in most men's, and yet not voluntarily kept, but inseparable from its very nature. I would gladly tell all that I know about it, and never paint "No Admittance" on my gate. (*Walden*, ch. 1)

Since mystical experiences are a feature of brain chemistry, not specific religions, atheists and agnostics have no particular reason to pooh-pooh the idea. As a matter of fact, mystical experience doesn't need a religious component at all, as demonstrated by the work of psychologist Mihaly Csikszentmihalyi, who introduced the notion of "flow" experience. Csikszentmihalyi found "flow" in experiences as diverse as sports and video gaming. He lists the elements likely to bring on flow experiences:

1. intense and focused concentration on the present moment;
2. merging of action and awareness;
3. a loss of reflective self-consciousness;
4. a sense of personal control or agency over the situation or activity;
5. a distortion of temporal experience; one's subjective experience of time is altered;
6. experience of the activity as intrinsically rewarding, also referred to as autotelic experience.[1]

---

1. As cited at http://en.wikipedia.org/wiki/Flow_(psychology).

A flow experience sounds like a mystical experience, doesn't it? Sounds nice, doesn't it? Furthermore, there's nothing mysterious about it. You can put yourself in the way of the flow experience by following very simple (and secular!) procedures.

Over the years, I have discovered that meditation and writing have the same effect: they bring my mind into the present moment. Buddhism teaches that when we are not living in the present moment, we are living in fantasy. We are out of touch with what is. Needless to say, when our minds are dwelling on the past or the future, we are also a long way from a mystical experience!

The feelings are the same; what we carry away from the mystical experience depends upon the stories we carry into it. The individual mystical experience is subjective and is most often meaningful only for the individual having the experience. For others, however, such as Moses or the Buddha or a long list of religious, artistic, and political people, the experience can trigger a personal transformation that has meaning for millions of others.

Why Does a Super-Nice Word Like "Spiritual" Make Humanists All Itchy?

Here is what Plato had to say about the body and the soul:

> Does not purification consist in this . . . in separating as much as possible the soul from the body, and in accustoming it to gather and collect itself by itself on all sides apart from the body, and to dwell, so far as it can, both now and hereafter, alone by itself, delivered, as it were, from the shackles of the body?[1]

Body and soul. Separate. The body impure . . . the thing that drives our poor, innocent souls to sex, selfishness, and overindulgence. The soul, that eternal, heaven-hungry thing; that incredible, detachable part of ourselves that will live in bliss forever . . . if only it can first conquer and then separate from that nasty, nasty body.

That's the thinking that drove the Western world all through the reign of Christendom. It fills the parking lots of megachurches to this day. Reinforcing that body/soul dichotomy is why the early Christians worked so hard to stamp out the philosophy of Epicurus, whose philosophy would nowadays be called "secular moral realism," a naturalistic worldview.

The dualists did a good job. The term "Epicurean" still has negative connotations.

For Plato and the Platonists, it's all about a disembodied soul and the next world. For Epicurus and the Epicureans, it's all about the connection of body and consciousness in this world, now. This very old argument between two very different worldviews is why the word "spiritual" makes so many humanists nervous. It implies the continuation of an age-old argument in the Western tradition—that of separating the physical from the spiritual, head from heart. For the past two and a half millennia, naturalists have lost the fight. (But whose bitter?) Naturalists are still here insisting that there is no separation between our thoughts and our bodies, that all our thoughts are embodied thoughts necessarily.

---

1. From *Phaedo*, in Plato, *Select Dialogues*.

The Varieties of Humanism

When we die, as Epicurus put it, our atoms disperse.

I don't know who's correct—or even if the question is an either/or—but entertaining clear dichotomies clarifies thinking. And this dialectic brings into bold relief the bigger question—the basic question of religion or philosophy: How should I live my life?

Am I living my life in order to prepare for the next one by keep my soul pure, or to get it pure again? Or are my thoughts and actions part of a physical continuity—a self—that will cease when what we call "life" ceases?

Basic questions each of us does well to answer as best we can. Seriously: How should I live my life? How well do my commitments actually match my goals? What do I owe to my self, to my soul, to humanity, and to world?

Epicurus focused the question this way: "You are not master of tomorrow, yet you postpone your happiness. Life is wasted in procrastination." If human beings do indeed have a detachable soul, Plato was most likely right about what to do: get as far away from that body as possible.

However, the naturalist Epicurus taught that in order to live a good life we have to stop and think about it. Think it through. Look at the bigger picture. Humanists also get itchy around the word "spiritual" when it comes before "practice," but whatever you call it, we all need it.

The Epicureans and the Stoics and the Buddhists were all very suspicious of what we nowadays call "self-talk." This inner dialogue very clearly creates our attitudes about our lives, yet, is the self-talk constructive, or even coherent, for that matter?

Might it be lying to us?

For these meditative traditions, that is the point of daily practice—getting hold of our self-talk and giving it direction.

At its essence, the spiritual exercise of meditation is about taking some time out of time to have a deep conversation with yourself, an inner dialogue. Meditation enables us to talk with ourselves, and—the most difficult challenge of all—in meditation we sometimes actually *listen* to ourselves and find our arguments convincing!

You are not master of tomorrow. How about sitting down and having a talk with yourself about that?

The Rise of the Totally Awesome "Whatever" God

"Moralistic Therapeutic Deism." That's the term sociologists Christian Smith and Melinda Lundquist Denton coined to describe the religious beliefs of the average North American. Reverend Robert Vinciguerra calls it "Egonovism," a neologism constructed of "ego" and "novo" (new). Reverend Rob claims that most Americans are Egonovists, even though most don't know it.[1]

Why are they saying such things? Here's one reason: Something on the order of 80 percent of Americans claim to be Christian, but 25 percent of Americans believe in reincarnation and 20 percent believe in karma—decidedly *un*Christian concepts. Such statistics tell us that Americans have gone way beyond "cafeteria Christianity" in our "spiritual but not religious" zeitgeist.

The Wikipedia article on Moralistic Therapeutic Deism summarizes its component beliefs:

1. "A god exists who created and ordered the world and watches over human life on Earth." (Note: This point alone disqualifies the system as deist. Deists believe there was a god who was the prime mover at the beginning of the universe, but that god is now hands-off.)

2. "God wants people to be good, nice, and fair to each other, as taught in the Bible and by most world religions."

3. "The central goal of life is to be happy and to feel good about oneself." (Rather a far cry from the old Christian hymn that intoned "such a worm as I.")

4. "God does not need to be particularly involved in one's life except when God is needed to resolve a problem." (Apparently, Jesus was confused about that "numbering the hairs on your head" thing.)

5. "Good people go to heaven when they die."

---

1. Vinciguerra, "Continued Observations on the Egonovism of American Society."

Sounds nice, doesn't it? Which is the first tip-off that something may be wrong here. How likely is it that the same god who smote the Egyptians is cool with whatever . . . and shoveling out favors?

Doesn't this list sound like wish fulfillment at its best?—an ATM god who awaits our every whim and clearly loves the wealthy more than the poor, underwriting an unjust economic and social system that happens to be handing out bennies to lucky me.

And, while this god is reloading the ATM, I'm free to do as I like if I'm nice.

As Rev. Bob's "ego" in Egonovism points out, this theology has an "I" problem, doesn't it? Whoever I am and whatever I'm doing is just fine with this god.

If you have read this far, it's not likely you are a Moralistic Therapeutic Deist or even a Deistic Moral Relativist. After all, an Egonovist won't be convinced by logic or reference to theology at all, because an important aspect of Egonovism is that it requires no pondering. No daily devotion. No sacrifice. The Egonovist god merely sits . . . or waits . . . somewhere, ready to dish out bennies to me.

None of that "straight is the gate and narrow is the way" stuff.

Sorry to sound like a Calvinist or something, but am I the only one who'd like to see Jesus make himself a "whip made of cords" and do some clearing of the temple here?

No, the money changers aren't going to be getting their tables kicked by the Egonovists.

The admission price to Egonovism is self-satisfaction and good ol'-fashioned hypocrisy.

Don't get me wrong: I think the moralistic therapeutic deity is as likely as any of the other gods human beings have thought up over time. Yet, I'm convinced that the point of religions is—and has always been—to stretch us, to call us to higher purposes than our basic lazy, selfish primate selves. Sure, religions also give teeth to social norms and underwrite whatever taboos a particular society has. Still, I can't help thinking the various gods who have asked for a little effort have played some positive role in human affairs.

The Egonovist god, not so much.

Makes me glad I'm a humanist!

That's Why They Call It "Practice"

When I was in my early twenties, I decided to dedicate myself to becoming a writer. Coming from a farming background, no one that I knew was a writer and no one that I knew had any idea about how to become a writer. (This was in the days before nearly every university and community college had a creative writing program.)

I decided to go study writing with one of my heroes, the Beat poet Allen Ginsberg. Ginsberg was at that time teaching at Naropa University in Boulder, Colorado, the first Buddhist university in the United States.

Ginsberg required his students to study meditation. As a young person with a lot of restless energy, I must admit that sitting *zazen* for an hour at a time was excruciating. I liked walking meditation considerably better. I kept at it despite my boredom.

Ginsberg taught that the writing of poetry itself is a meditative practice. A discipline. A way of getting into the here and now and quieting down. So, since 1982, I have sat down every morning, if at all possible, and taken a few breaths and meditated. Then I write. As with Buddhist meditation, writing can be a way to focus on the present moment, the here and now.

I keep in mind the advice of the Roman poet Horace, who said, *Nulla dies sine linea*—"Never a day without a line." With more than thirty years of such practice, you can imagine that I've written quite a few lines.

Any time anyone asks me about being a writer, I always advise sitting down every day at the same time of day and writing for at least an hour. It's a practice, a routine. I advise the same thing for anyone who asks me about meditation—sit down and do it, the same time every day.

What's the point? Reaching equanimity, compassion, and wisdom. This has always been the point. From the Daoists to the Buddhists to the Stoics to the latest strip-mall fad.

As I have said before in this book, I think the Stoic philosopher Marcus Aurelius perhaps best stated the task:

> Always keep in mind the nature of the universe and the nature or your own nature and how the one relates to the other and what

being a part of the entire universe means. Remember that no one can stop you from doing and saying those things which are your part in the universe.

Oh, do I have to? Marcus says it's a darn good idea if you're going to have any depth of character at all:

> Do all the problems of the world distract you? Give yourself time to learn something new and good. Stop being whirled around. Shallow people tire themselves by doing, doing, and yet have no goal toward which to direct their movements or their thoughts.[1]

That's straightforward, isn't it?

Marcus puts it even more succinctly: "Those who do not observe the movements of their own minds must of necessity be unhappy."

Daily practice. It's not rocket science. And it's not about expensive retreats or exotic positions. It's about taking some time to get into the moment, looking at the reality that surrounds us, and looking at the movement of our own minds. You don't have to be a Stoic or a Buddhist or any other "ist" or "ism." Marcus Aurelius points to a simple way: "Always keep in mind the nature of the whole and your own nature and how the one relates to the other and what being a part of the whole means."

Because "those who do not observe the movements of their own minds must of necessity be unhappy."[2]

That's very wise.

---

1. *Meditations*, II.9, 7 (author's translation).
2. Ibid., II.8 (author's translation).

You Might Be a Religious Naturalist

> Be anxious for nothing, but in everything, by prayer and petition, with thanksgiving, present your requests to God.
> —Philippians 4:5 (Berean Study Bible)

The *Dictionary of Philosophy and Religion* defines religion this way:

> From the Latin *relegare* ("to bind fast"), typically the term refers to an institution with a recognized body of communicants who gather together regularly for worship, and accept a set of doctrines offering some means of relating the individual to what is taken to be the ultimate nature of reality.[1]

Wikipedia defines it this way:

> Religion is a cultural system of behaviors and practices, world views, ethics, and social organization that relate humanity to an order of existence.[2]

Both definitions contain the idea that religion exists (1) as a community and (2) as an orientation of the human toward something greater.

Wisely, the second definition leaves out the bit about "worship," a word that makes sense in only some religions. The second definition is one that humanists can sink our teeth into. In this sense, humanism is a religion. And, in this sense, religious naturalism is one orientation that humanism can take—an orientation that dismisses some of the time-worn objections to humanism—stuff about heads and rationalism and all that.

I define religious naturalism this way: a community of people who hold that that which is greater, the cosmos, is best grasped through the scientific method.

---

1. Reese, ed., *Dictionary of Philosophy and Religion*, "religion."
2. https://en.wikipedia.org/Wiki/Religion.

The Varieties of Humanism

You might be a religious naturalist if you think that neither time nor the universe has any interest in . . . you, or the American electorate. Or the United States. Or even humankind. Because, well, another news flash: The sun will burn out. This planet will go dark. And, eventually, something will happen to the universe—a Big Crunch, heat death, something. And time will be no more.

That's the bad news. The good news is that we are here, now. Together. That's the essence of what science tells us of the universe and its destiny. I find it a considerably more hopeful story than any of the ones containing anthropomorphized gods or angels.

∽

Ah, but what about awe and wonder?

I'll tell you a story about the sublime. I heard this from a friend. He was a chain-smoker, and he coughed through all of his stories. He had a couple of degrees in English literature, and he had been in Vietnam. There he'd had a desk job well away from the fighting. But one night he found himself out on a road, away from the city lights. On the horizon, he saw B-52 bombers attacking a village. The entire horizon lit up with the explosions. He thought to himself, "My god, how beautiful!" Then he thought about the hundreds of people under those bombs—human beings having their loved ones, all they owned, and their lives taken away from them.

My friend waved his cigarette at me and said, "It was sublime." Like many who have seen such things, before and after, he drank himself to death trying to come to terms with what he had seen and thought.

The sublime. The word is derived from Latin: *sub*, "up to," and *limus*, "threshold." (*Limus* is also where we get the term "liminal," the space between.) So "sublime" is all the way up to the limit ("limit" being another word derived from *limitare*.)

My friend knew the definition of "sublime." He had been up to the limit; he had experienced the threshold, the edge, the place where terror and awe meet.

We often hear that one god or another is the key to wonder and awe, which we hear is the essence of the religious experience. The etymology of "awe" reveals that terror and dread are at the root of the word. This emotion can perhaps be better described by the word "sublime."

It was the sublime, the edge of terror and awe, that drove the Hebrew prophets to prophecy. It was this edge that my friend experienced.

Terror mixed with awe is the basis for what has come to be called the "overview effect," defined as a cognitive shift caused among those who see the Earth from space. (The first evidence of this effect is the NASA photograph *Earthrise*, taken from lunar orbit in 1968.) But the mystics among us know that we don't have to go to outer space to experience the overview effect. It occurs to everyone during what we call "transcendental experiences."

You might be a religious naturalist if you have experienced the sublime outside of conventional religious practice.

∽

Here are some questions I find useful to ask when thinking about religion:

> What do human beings want from a deity?
> What do human beings want from a religion?
> What do human beings want from life?
> Are what human beings want from a deity and a religion similar to what we want from a life?

As is the case with many questions, the way I go about asking these basic questions guides the answers I get: the bias of my questions comes from my assumption that deity—at any rate, deity as presented in most religions—is a creation of human beings, not the other way around.

The opposite assumption is that deity exists and human beings are left to figure out "the will of God" based somewhat on personal revelation but mostly on one scripture and tradition or another. This belief has been the bias of many, many theologians through time. Those fragments that they have shored against their ruins, as T. S. Eliot put it, make up most of the human theological project. As a humanist, I begin from the other way around.

Again, my questions:

> What do human beings want from a deity?
> What do human beings want from a religion?
> What do human beings want from life?
> Are what human beings want from a deity and a religion similar to what we want from a life?

My answer to the last question is yes—what human beings want from a deity and a religion are similar—I would say identical—to what we want in a life. These "asks" boil down to four things:

- To counteract the apparent danger and chaos of human existence.

The Varieties of Humanism

- To give an apparent direction to the chaos of reality.
- To underwrite or guarantee the meaning and purpose of life.
- To insure the transcendent: that life and death have meaning.

⌒

Allow me to take for example the religion of my youth, a movement known as Oneness Pentecostalism. In that belief system, there is only one God—the Trinity of orthodox Christianity has been rejected. To simplify a bit, Jesus is God. This God has always existed and will always exist and is omniscient, omnipotent, and omnipresent—all-knowing, all-powerful, and everywhere all the time. In answer to the question, "Why do bad things happen to good people?," Oneness Pentecostals will answer that we human beings, who are clearly limited in our knowledge, power, and location, simply can't know—or comprehend—the will of God. However, says Oneness Pentecostal teaching, what we can know is that God has everything under control and that everything that happens, happens for a reason. Our part in the drama of human existence is to "trust and obey." Even if our lives are grim, we can count on a bright eternity coming "on the other side."

I am not denigrating this way of thinking. It answers those questions I asked initially:

> What do human beings want from a deity?
> What do human beings want from a religion?
> What do human beings want from life?
> Are what human beings want from a deity and a religion similar to what we want from a life?

The answers: Oneness Pentecostalism says that God has everything under control. The meaning and purpose of life is to obey this mighty God. By so doing, there is no chaos in human existence, despite its many dangers. All events are directed by God.

The Oneness Pentecostal God is what theologians call "transcendent": above and beyond the natural, observable universe. Most of the people I've known and loved in my life have lived in the assurances of this theology. I have found, however, that I cannot live with these beliefs. This fact has made me a seeker after other truths.

If you have trod a similar path, you might be a religious naturalist.

⌒

The traditionally religious—at least those who believe in the sciences—find themselves continually in the "god of the gaps" problem: that what we don't know continues to shrink.

Early in twentieth century the Unitarian minister John Haynes Holmes said, "The supernatural is everywhere giving way to the natural." From a Western prospective, this appeared to be the case—onward and upward and all that. Early humanist leaders such as John Dietrich, Curtis Reese, and Charles F. Potter agreed with Holmes's assessment, and they explored ways to carry those aspects of religion that they thought of as positive into the coming secular age.

This was the beginning of the contemporary religious naturalism movement, based on the older notions of deism and transcendentalism. It is in that tradition that I frame how I ask and how I answer those questions I began with:

> What do human beings want from a deity?
> What do human beings want from a religion?
> What do human beings want from life?
> Are what human beings want from a deity and a religion similar to what we want from a life?

Here are my own answers to these questions:

What human beings want in a deity and what deity might be perhaps have little or nothing in common. For this reason many people have intuitively understood that a subjectively satisfying deity must be a "personal Jesus" or a "personal relationship with God." Again, that insight works for those for whom it works. This does not work for me, and you might be a religious naturalist if it doesn't work for you.

That a god or gods exist that would supply individual needs or answer individual prayers seems nonsensical and even morally offensive to me. A deity that would answer the prayers of the wealthy, for example, and ignore the entreaties of the poor, is an evil god. The only logical way that I can see to say that deity has any morality is to say that deity has little or no ability or opportunity to answer entreaties.

As to the question of a direction to reality and a guarantee to life having a meaning and purpose: To say that human history has had a direction is to ignore human history. The suffering and slaughter of history does not add up to the happy, advanced days of the present state of the world. The world is not in a happy or advanced state for most of the human beings alive on the planet—never has been and apparently never will be. We must not fall into the trap of thinking our own time is unique and in any way the "crown of creation."

***

As to meaning and purpose: the simplest way to frame the question is, why would a universe (and perhaps multiverses exist), why would reality, have a human meaning and purpose? That idea comes from a time when human beings understood the Earth as a central part of the cosmos. Now we know that isn't true.

To the question of transcendence—that every life and death has meaning—the religious naturalist and humanist answer is that meaning and purpose are created by human beings. Just so, every life and every death (however short the life and however tragic the death) has meaning if we, together, insist that every life and every death has meaning.

Again, I am speaking for myself, out of the tradition of humanism and religious naturalism. The tradition represented by John Haynes Holmes when he said, "The supernatural is everywhere giving way to the natural."

If what I'm saying makes sense, you might be a religious naturalist too.

***

It's straightforward: death is the irreducible fact. The loss of our own consciousness, the loss of a loved one . . . death is terrible. It is the irreducible fact of existence. From organic compounds, to molecules, to living cells, to primates . . . life wills itself. Pushes. Insists. Creates. Then violence or accident or illness or age destroy that will to life . . .

Death is the natural outcome of a natural process, yet it feels so unnatural, so wrong.

To counter this irreducible fact of death, we have invented reductions: We say, "It is not . . ." or "It is only . . ." We call it "passing." We try desperately to reduce death. Still, despite the stories, the denials, death remains the irreducible fact.

When we realize this—and after we stop the stories—we find ourselves free of superstition. Then we are ready, at last, to look down at the Earth and up at the stars and see them for the first time. If this place is where you find yourself, you might be a religious naturalist.

***

But isn't all of this naturalism a bit . . . pedestrian and depressing?

It is according to how much you want to know how things really are. I for one prefer the scientific story of billions of years of evolution to the story of a god with curiously human characteristics creating Earth and its flora and fauna in a week or so.

I prefer the belief that it's up to each of us to decide to do and be good to the belief that if we don't act right we will be punished by eternal and almighty forces.

If you agree, you might be a religious naturalist.

⁓

But what about feelings and emotions? Isn't religious naturalism cold and logical?

The question of rationality goes way back. Let's be clear: every human being thinks emotionally first, reasonably second. It's that "fight or flight" mechanism.

Every human being is first and foremost a creature of emotion. Every person is a potential artist, poet, lover, and there are aspects of our psyche that thrive best in the artistic, poet, lover mode. The question is about remaining there.

Ancient philosophers realized that rationality is not our default mode. But it is useful. Religious naturalists choose to know rather than to believe.

I look at it this way: One reason that food banks prefer money to food donations is that people who go to the grocery store to buy food for a food bank will, rather than buying what they would buy for themselves, try to *think* about what poor people want to eat. As a result, they tend to buy fatty, salty foods rather than healthy ones. Just so, I think many people who have concluded that there probably isn't a god continue to say they do believe, because they are protecting people they see as disadvantaged and therefore in need of a god.

If you are tired of faking it, you might be a religious naturalist.

⁓

You might be a religious naturalist if you place your highest trust in that which can be proven; if you think that science describes reality. If you think that to trust in science is to trust in human community and the human project. If you think that science is systematic and testable in an international community.

You might be a religious naturalist if you suspect that supernatural beliefs are most likely untrue.

The Varieties of Humanism

You might be a religious naturalist if you think that the problems created by concepts such as god, souls, and an afterlife vastly outnumber the solutions such explanations offer.

You might be a religious naturalist if you are inclined to think that, far from being a reason for despair, the realization that there is no deity granting requests and no meaning or purpose outside of the human mind frees us to ask questions rather than follow preconceived formulas.

You might be a religious naturalist if you ask yourself, "What can I do in my short life that will benefit the human project?"

The realization that all meaning and purpose is a product of the human mind and human culture enables individuals to question the culture, the status quo, and offer alternatives. Pluralistic, creative societies are the result.

Furthermore, we don't have to buy the belief so common in medieval and early-modern Europe that each of us has a predetermined and proper place in society. We can rebel against the social class we were born into and even against the very foundations of society.

Awareness—deep awareness—does not lead to endless ecstatic bliss. But it does lead to integrity and authenticity. The human condition—the cosmic condition—is both tragic and comic. It is sublime.

If you agree, you might be a religious naturalist.

༄

"Don't you worry 'bout a thing," wrote Stevie Wonder. So did Paul in his Epistle to the Philippians. "Be anxious for nothing," Paul wrote. Why? How? Paul's answer was "prayer and petition" while giving thanks to God. For many alive on this planet, that answer still works.

Others of us see no evidence for believing that petitions or prayers get answered. Still, we are not anxious. We trust the cosmos to be as it appears to be.

If you see as we do, you too may be a religious naturalist.

Religion:
It's What You Do

Have you ever noticed how pointless it is to ask someone, "What's your religion?" The answer is likely to be a proper noun, such as Baptist or Hindu. But what does that designation mean to the person answering the question? Does such an answer tell us anything? Beyond, perhaps, an origin for someone's recent gene pool or perhaps about some idiosyncratic choices?

Separating out religion from everything else we do—all the other meaning-making systems we use—is only a convenience. As anthropologist Jonathan Z. Smith put it,

> Religion is solely the creation of the scholar's study. It is created for the scholar's analytic purposes by his imaginative acts of comparison and generalization. Religion has no existence apart from the academy.[1]

Allowing for humor and rhetorical overstatement, Professor Smith's point is that we exist in a matrix of symbolic systems that we separate out only for the sake of contemplation (and, perhaps, clarification).

In our minds—and in our lives—the meanings are all mashed up, a puree or whip of meaning and purpose . . . Is it about morals? ethics? politics? personal integrity?

It's always about all of the above. And the below. And the between.

Human beings are meaning-making creatures. We manage to make the meanings we make in systems of narrative and symbol, some of which we understand, most of which most of us don't.

In these systems, it's us or them: we control them, or they control us. Whenever we aren't paying attention, it is the latter.

Given this mushy, mashy matrix in which we create the meaning in our lives, removing what is conventionally called "religious" (or "spiritual") from a personal or collective meaning-making system does not leave a hole

---

1. Smith, *Imagining Religion*, 200.

or gap, but is rather an opening that other symbolic systems will fill by other means. Or, more probably, the same means by different names.

Religion isn't a thing; it's a way of thinking. When we pay attention. When we don't, religion is just another excuse.

Within the Western tradition, "god" still packs a meaningful punch to many people, especially North Americans. Yet, if the god-concept does not guarantee or underwrite meaning and purpose for you or me, something else will . . . perhaps even the insistence that life has meaning and purpose without the god-concept!

Think for a moment about how many people you know who take meaning and purpose from their concept of god. Does it change their way of being in the world? My suspicion is that the concept usually functions as shorthand for something else in most human lives. Theologian Gordon D. Kaufman puts it this way:

> The central question for theology is not . . . primarily a speculative question, a problem of knowledge at all. Most fundamentally it is a practical question: How are we to live? To what should we devote ourselves? To what cause give ourselves? Put in religious terms: How can we truly serve God? What is proper worship?[2]

Put succinctly: "What's your cause?" Your cause may be survival. Or approval. Family. World peace. Lots of things.

Often the god-concept becomes the straw man who underwrites pre-existing wishes and prejudices.

The symbolic systems we live in are difficult to see and even more difficult to separate into understandable strands. Most difficult of all is putting all the strands back into a conceivable whole. Yet, finally, there is no religion, no politics, no self. Only the forest of symbols and stories we wander in.

As Jean-Paul Sartre once said, "Freedom is what you do with what's been done to you."

Freedom is also figuring out why we do what we do.

---

2. Kaufman, *In Face of Mystery*, 15–16.

5

What's the Humanist Mission?

> There is no time for messing around. You have been retained as counsel for the unhappy. You have promised to bring help to the shipwrecked, the imprisoned, the sick, the needy, to those whose heads are under the poised axe. What are you thinking about instead? What are you doing?
>
> —SENECA

The Wrath of Pew

Another Pew poll showing another major decline in church attendance appeared this week. This is becoming a habit! The 2015 poll shows church attendance is down nearly 8 percent since the 2007 poll that had us all talking. And that mysterious group we hadn't heard of until 2007, the "nones," increased from 16 percent of Americans in the previous poll to nearly 24 percent. No religion. None. And no plans of finding one, at least in the traditional denominations. And you know, I must say it's all good.

I say that not because I'm a humanist indulging in schadenfreude, but because I'm an American with some hopes for the future.

I recently read *The Road to Character* by conservative *New York Times* columnist David Brooks. The book sits at number two on the *New York Times* bestseller list for nonfiction. It's a good book. It's not a conservative's panacea, as was a previous bestseller, *The Closing of the American Mind*. Allan Bloom's book was target practice on straw men. Brooks is inadvertently showing us why traditional religion is in free fall in the US.

Brooks sets out on his exploration of how we develop character by distinguishing between "resume virtues" and "eulogy virtues"—that is, those things we do to survive and thrive in the culture we find ourselves in, and those things we do that we are remembered for after our deaths. Brooks says, "We live in a society that encourages us to think about how to have a great career but leaves many of us inarticulate about how to cultivate the inner life." Interesting: a majority-Christian culture inarticulate about cultivating an inner life. Churches flubbed their chance.

Easily retaining his title as "the liberal's favorite conservative," Brooks explores the lives of personalities as diverse as Dwight Eisenhower and Mary Ann Evans, the Victorian radical Unitarian better known by her pen name, George Eliot.

I think Brooks gets it right when he claims that we live a "life of vague moral aspiration." Mainline religions stand accused. It sounds like an accusation echoing right out of the Victorian era, and it reminds me of that paragon of Victorian Unitarian values, Rev. James Freeman Clarke, and his famous—even infamous now—"salvation by character."

Reverend Clarke would no doubt have packed up his duds and joined Brooks on the road to character. The idea that our characters can always use some work is far from being a quaint Victorian sentiment or a conservative hobbyhorse. It is the unstated but driving force behind many popular movements in contemporary culture that are replacements for flaccid Christianity, from yoga and mindfulness to neo-Stoicism and renewed interest in Epicureanism. As poll after poll shows the collapse of mainline Christianity and the rise of "nones" and the "spiritual but not religious," books and classes that promise paths to character development will no doubt proliferate like kudzu.

Contemporary writer Joan Didion defined character as "the willingness to accept responsibility for one's own life." Didion and James Freeman Clarke underline something that we too often forget nowadays: that the purpose of inner work, the work of building character, is to accomplish outward work, the work of compassion and social justice. As David Brooks puts it, "The ultimate joys are moral joys." Joy and character. This is what many of those missing from the pews have hit the road searching for.

What does the man who would become St. Augustine and the woman who would become George Eliot have in common? According to Brooks, both show a willingness to do the inner work that turns to external good for humanity. Both found a road to character outside of the norms of their day. George Eliot perhaps sums that road up best: "It's never too late to be what you might have been."

Life, Liberty, and the Pursuit of . . . What?

Think for a moment about what happiness means to you. Not what happiness is supposed to mean to you—"happiness is a warm puppy," "happiness is a warm gun" . . . happiness is sex, drugs, and rock 'n' roll, et cetera, et cetera—but what happiness means to you.

What makes you happy? Where is your happy place?

Hold on to that idea, if you will, as we examine what pursuing happiness looks like. As you cogitate, ask yourself this question: Is being happy my goal in life?

In his novel *Nicholas Nickleby*, Charles Dickens wrote, "Happiness is a gift and the trick is not to expect it, but to delight in it when it comes." Do you agree with that? That's one way of thinking about happiness—a happy accident.

On a dourer note, novelist Thomas Hardy wrote in *The Mayor of Casterbridge*, "Happiness was but the occasional episode in a general drama of pain." Is *that* your view of life?

Both British writers are working with an older view of happiness, based on the word's origin—from the Middle English *hap*, meaning luck or chance. "Mayhap" means possibly.

The more common English word nowadays is "perhaps," meaning . . . maybe. Which, you see, connects back to the older "mayhap." The most common derivative of *hap* is "hap-pen"—something that takes place—mixing in the older understanding that occurrences happen by chance.

But that isn't what we mean by "happiness" when we are out there looking for it, is it? Happiness is something to be pursued. Chased. Achieved. It doesn't just hap-pen.

When he drafted the Declaration of Independence, Thomas Jefferson posited three "unalienable rights": "life, liberty, and the pursuit of happiness." He didn't mean "life, liberty, and the pursuit of whatever happens to happen," did he?

Or, did he?

What's the Humanist Mission?

Did he mean that citizens have the right to "life, liberty, and perhaps, maybe getting lucky"?

> We hold these truths to be self-evident, that all men are created equal, that they are endowed by their Creator with certain unalienable Rights, that among these are Life, Liberty, and the pursuit of Happiness.

United States citizens theoretically have these rights, but the devil is always in the details. Jefferson's words make an argument from natural law—that the nature of reality itself makes these rights "self-evident." Thomas Jefferson, the chief author of the Declaration of Independence, was canny in his argument. He does not quote chapter and verse from the Bible. He does not cite tradition or common law. Who or what the "Creator" is gets no definition or explanation. It is the truths that he is asserting, not the source of truth.

Why it was not also self-evident that women, or slaves, or natives were equally endowed with these rights gets no mention. The problem with the document is that it is not in any way a Declaration of Universal Rights—it's only concerned with a narrow slice of the population.

Still, these are radical words. And these words point toward a reality that has not yet been achieved in the US but is a goal to be striven for nonetheless.

What it means to pursue happiness is the greatest disconnect between what the nation could be and what it is. *Black's Law Dictionary* defines the phrase "pursuit of happiness" in constitutional law:

> a right that includes personal freedom; freedom of contract; exemption from oppression or invidious discrimination; the right to follow one's individual preference in the choice of an occupation and the application of his energies; liberty of conscience; and the right to enjoy domestic relations and the privileges of the family and home.[1]

All very good to have. No doubt these are even essential rights, but Jefferson had considerably more in mind. He wasn't about merely handing citizens a hunting license and a pat on the back—"Good luck, citizen. Hope you get lucky."

---

1. *Black's Law Dictionary*, "Pursuit of happiness."

Doctor Carol Ryff is a psychologist best known for having developed the Ryff Scale of Psychological Well-Being. She claims that happiness consists of six things:

1. Autonomy
2. Personal growth
3. Self-acceptance
4. Purpose in life
5. Environmental mastery
6. Positive relations with others

The rights guaranteed by the constitutional definition of "pursuit of happiness" are necessary to these factors, but not sufficient. In other words, Americans have the right to pursue happiness but many—if not most—citizens are not supplied with the tools to catch it. Many don't have the means to achieve the rights they have, and that is an injustice.

I've spent this past week on jury duty, and I was reminded of a quip by Winston Churchill, who said, "The best argument against democracy is a five-minute conversation with the average voter."

Clever. But unfortunately true.

How might we make a conversation with the average voter a *good* argument for democracy? That, I think, is what Jefferson had in mind by "pursuit of happiness." And we in this nation have not sought that goal for everyone.

Perhaps you've heard that the Dali Lama and Bishop Desmond Tutu have agreed to write a book together called *The Book of Joy*, about "finding enduring happiness in an uncertain world." Doug Abrams, who has been contracted to pull the book together, says,

> While happiness is often seen as being dependent on external circumstances, His Holiness and the Archbishop believe that joy comes from an internal state of being. They will share how joy animates our lives and leads ultimately to a life of greater meaning and purpose and greater love and contribution.

I look forward to the book. But Thomas Jefferson already wrote that book for us. In the Declaration of Independence Jefferson was making a very humanist argument. He was putting first things first. The first thing is to know why we are doing something. This act of thinking things through

What's the Humanist Mission?

from their foundation to their completion, and then being able to act on our thinking, is what Jefferson meant by "the pursuit of happiness." It's about meaning and purpose.

Spoiler alert for the Dali Lama's book: happiness is not pursued by acquiring things; happiness is pursued in thinking about what the first thing is that one should put first. It is the pursuit of that thing in knowledge and wisdom.

Imagine for a moment a scenario in which every American citizen has the right to the ability and the leisure time to think things through. This was Jefferson's ideal: a nation of citizens equipped and able to think things through.

How many of the signers of the Declaration of Independence had a similar thought in mind? Probably very few. The problem lies in the fact that the word "happiness" is a poor translation of what the Greek philosopher Epicurus (342–270 BCE) had in mind.

The phrase "life, liberty, and the pursuit of happiness" is unique to the draft of the Declaration that Jefferson wrote. The phrase is based on the work of the British philosopher John Locke, except that Locke wrote "life, liberty, and property."

"Life, liberty, and property" makes a lot more sense as things government might guarantee, and the constitutional law definition uses this property idea, but we have to assume that Jefferson wasn't confused. He didn't accidentally change the words to "pursuit of happiness" instead of "property."

The key, I think, lies in a letter Jefferson wrote to William Short in 1819. William Short was at one time Jefferson's personal secretary and also served in ambassadorial roles in Europe. Their relationship was so close that Jefferson referred to Short as an "adoptive son." Jefferson wrote to Short,

> As you say of yourself, I TOO AM AN EPICUREAN. I consider the genuine (not the imputed) doctrines of Epicurus as containing every thing rational in moral philosophy which Greece and Rome have left us.

"I too am an Epicurean." Jefferson quickly added "the genuine (not the imputed) doctrines of Epicurus."

Jefferson said of Epicurus that his work contains "every thing rational in moral philosophy which Greece and Rome have left us." Quite a compliment, considering the high regard the founders had for Greece and Rome.

But it's also telling that Jefferson didn't say "political philosophy." He said "moral philosophy."

The fact that he said "moral philosophy" indicates that Jefferson was being considerably more subversive in the Declaration than he is given credit for. He was hiding an Easter egg, if you will, a beautiful bomb, in the composition that has yet to explode.

Epicurus started with what he saw as a "first thing first." What do human beings want? Epicurus asked. His answer: we want, first and foremost, to minimize pain and maximize pleasure. Epicurus gets accused of hedonism for saying such a thing, but, again, this is about a first principle. A place to start considering the good in human life. He said,

> A clear understanding of desires enables us to base every choice and avoidance upon whether it secures or upsets bodily comfort and peace of mind, which is the goal of a happy life.

"Every choice"? That requires a lot of thought. Epicurus wrote, "Wisdom is the beginning and end of a happy life."

Wisdom? Ick. Where's the sex, drugs, and rock 'n' roll in that? Which is exactly the point.

The sort of happiness Epicurus had in mind is not something for sale on eBay. Or at the Galleria. Not something to be had through sex, money, power, a good address, or cheesecake. In the meaning that Epicurus and Jefferson were using, it doesn't have anything to do with luck, either. It's about a citizen having the time and ability to decide what matters—what meaning and purpose mean.

"Happiness" is an unfortunate translation of the Greek word *eudaimonia*, a combination of two words: *eu*, meaning "good," and *daimon*, meaning "spirit." A good spirit. Though the word is often translated into English as "happiness," a better translation is probably "human flourishing."

Does eating this piece of cheesecake bring me comfort and peace of mind? Does it aid human flourishing? Well, as a matter of fact it might! In addition, my having this piece of cheesecake doesn't hurt anyone else. Well, then, do it.

However, we also know that eating too much cheesecake, or drinking too much, et cetera, et cetera, also brings pain—as type 2 diabetes, which is a pain rather than pleasure and, in addition, is not a comfort and does not contribute to peace of mind.

OK. Don't do that.

Sounds like I need to moderate my intake of cheesecake. That's why Epicurus wasn't an Epicurean in the common understanding of the term. According to Epicurus this chain of thinking leads to *arete*, a word often translated into English as "virtue," but that term has lots of baggage from its use in Christianity. It's probably best translated into English as "fulfillment," which, by golly, brings us happiness, doesn't it? Fulfillment. That's a good thing!

Practical philosophy works like that. It encourages us to think through the little things in order to see how they become the big things. Practical philosophy, like theology in religions, pushes us toward looking at the small questions as connected to the biggest question, the question of what gives meaning and purpose to life.

Yes, where we stand on eating cheesecake or drinking or smoking or consuming, et cetera is ultimately how we live our lives. Momentary happiness is not ultimate and sustainable happiness. And individual (me, me, mine) happiness is not human flourishing for everybody else. It is a cause of human suffering rather than a remedy.

In his explication of Epicurus, Jefferson wrote, "To procure tranquility of mind we must avoid desire and fear, the two principal diseases of the mind."

Remember that I had you think about what happiness means to you . . . not what you've been told that happiness is by a culture built on convincing us we need stuff, more cheesecake, but what happiness means to you. What makes you happy? Where is your happy place?

That's important. And it's something to build a life on.

Finally, think about Winston Churchill's quip: "The best argument against democracy is a five-minute conversation with the average voter." We chuckle knowingly. The average voter doesn't really get democracy; but isn't that the failure of the nation, not of the citizen?

It's not likely that most people think of pursuing happiness as the right and ability to make rational decisions. But just think what it would mean to our society if that were a right and a duty . . .

What would it mean for every citizen to have the right to that pursuit of happiness?

Would it mean better education? Affordable higher education? Six-hour workdays? Thirty-hour work weeks? Eight weeks of paid vacation? What?

The fact is we don't know because we haven't even tried. That is the little egg, the little bomb Thomas Jefferson hid in plain sight. It has been ticking for a long time.

Perhaps someday it will explode.

Welcome to the Age of Practice

The first person to doubt... Did they doubt because of oppression, because of terror or grief, or just the opposite—because of some heady freedom, because of safety and joy?

Was perhaps the first person to doubt also the first to believe?

What is it in human consciousness that causes either? Are they intertwined, the one inevitably triggering its opposite in a perpetual dance?

How does the world we experience come into being and continue to exist? This is the question that has tickled the mind of human beings for some time now. Some are satisfied with the answer "unseen forces"; others are not. And on it goes—belief/doubt, doubt/belief.

For those convinced that the mysteries of being and becoming most likely lie in being and becoming itself, stories are necessary but not sufficient. Stories are extrapolations from reality but do not reflect the nature of experience itself; life doesn't have a plot, does it? Therefore, we know that all stories—and myths are stories—are inherently false.

So, how do we find order in our lives? After all, science and reason exist in and as stories too. This can blind us to the fact that science and reason come closer to approximating the being and becoming that eludes stories.

We could say that reason is a religion. That makes some sense. The Stoic philosopher Epictetus asked, "How long are you planning to wait to demand the best of yourself? How long will you act against reason?" Many thinkers have equated self-improvement and self-mastery with reason.

The twentieth-century philosopher Martin Heidegger—a somewhat reasonable man—enumerated three diseases of the soul:

> We forget that we are alive;
>
> we forget that everything is connected;
>
> we forget that we are free to live for ourselves.[1]

How do we remember these things? The need for this remembering—the need to reason concerning these matters—is why we live in the Age of

---

1. As described in School of Life, "Great Philosophers 10: Martin Heidegger."

Practice. Enough people have realized that the endless dance of belief and doubt does very little to improve the human condition, from the way we make it through a day to the way we sustain human society.

What do we mean by "meaning," and what would living a life of meaning look like? Back to Heidegger's trilogy:

> It is a life in which we remember that we are alive,
> a life in which we remember that everything is connected,
> a life in which we remember that we are free to live for ourselves.

It is a life of both differentiation and connection, a life of learning, and a life of service.

We reach this goal daily through a practice that teaches us to stop, stabilize, calm down, and notice the being and becoming that surrounds us.

There is nothing of the dance of belief and doubt in this. There is only being and becoming. Only action and reflection. There is only centering and noticing and remembering that we are alive and connected and free. Yes, there are contradictions in that sequence. But not insurmountable ones.

Confucian meditation is called *Chou Won*, a combination of the words meaning "sit" and "forget." The Stoic philosopher Marcus Aurelius put it this way:

> Always keep in mind the nature of the whole and your own nature and how the one relates to the other and what being a part of the whole means. Remember that no one can stop you from doing and saying those things which are your part in the whole.

And this:

> Does all the busyness distract you? Give yourself time to learn something new and good and stop being whirled around. The shallow weary themselves by doing, doing, and yet have no goal toward which to direct their movements or their thoughts.[2] (II.7)

Good call, Confucius. Good call, Marcus. The meaning is the practice.

---

2. *Meditations*, II.9, 7 (author's translation).

Martian Sleeper Cells and the Spiritual Practice of Science

Since I'm both a minister and a humanist, I'm asked—often in rather shocked terms—if I am an atheist. Many humanists use that label as a positive description rather than a negative one. After all, being labeled an a-theist implies that theism is somehow normative and that being outside that norm is an important qualifier. I don't identify as an atheist. I'm a post-theist.

Here's an analogy to clarify what I'm thinking: I recently bought a new Ford truck. I bought a Ford because it's good, solid, relatively efficient transportation. I also bought it because I have fond memories of Ford trucks—both my grandfathers had Ford trucks when I was a kid. Both had started buying Fords with the Model T.

I bought a new Ford truck, not a Model T. Why? Because a Model T, even though it revolutionized the automobile industry, is no long an efficient mode of transportation in the contemporary world.

Does that mean that I don't "believe" in the Model T? Am I an a-Model-T-ist? Not at all. I'm a post-Model-T-ist. I have no doubt that my new Ford truck is built upon knowledge gained in the manufacture of Model Ts. The Ford I drive today could not exist as it does without the Model T.

This is how I view "god." It's not that I don't believe in the god-concept. It's that I don't think the concept is "good transportation" in our contemporary context.

Yet, my analogy also "proves" just the opposite of my point, doesn't it? Because we could also say that my Ford truck is merely the latest version of the Model T, isn't it?

I'm not an a-theist. Nor am I an a-Model-T-ist.

Then there are always Subarus.

Philosophers Know What They Need

The story goes that a rich man asked the Greek philosopher Diogenes why it was that rich men do not follow philosophers but philosophers follow rich men. Diogenes replied, "Because philosophers know what they need; the rich do not."

What I know for sure is that we human beings need meaning and purpose in our lives. The question is where and how to find meaning and purpose. For me, a poet, meaning is generated in the creative act of noticing the moment and using the human creation of language to communicate that.

There are other methods.

Let's consider: What if I decide that life has meaning and purpose because I believe Martians invaded in 1865 and formed a sleeper cell that has now come awake in the guise of a popular reality television show? By watching this TV show, I believe, I receive messages from our Martian overlords, instructions as to what I should do.

Such a belief could without question give my life meaning and purpose. Each commercial break, for example, might indicate by the number of individual commercials how many bridges the Martians wish me to blow up. I have my marching orders; I have meaning and purpose.

That such a belief system gives me meaning and purpose is not debatable. Even that this belief system gives me more meaning and purpose than others I might have might be the case.

What is debatable is whether or not this particular form of meaning and purpose has value to the larger human community. This is the interface between my subjectivity and the objective world of others. Where the rubber meets the road, if you will.

Sure, if every human being on the planet agreed with my belief in a Martian sleeper cell, all of humanity would have meaning and purpose. So. Is mass delusion a positive good? Is it preferable to finding meaning and purpose in a more thoughtful way?

Is delusion "better" than relying upon more dependable methods that perhaps will fail at delivering a common meaning and purpose to large groups of people?

Here's another thing I think is true: meaning and purpose are human constructs and therefore can be constructed only by human beings. Why ever might we want a god or gods to construct meaning and purpose for us?

It's also clear from a cursory peek at human history that meaning and purpose take different forms at different times. Henry Ford didn't stick with his blockbuster Model T. He didn't arrogantly insist that what he had already found was successful enough. Instead, Ford shut down his factory and retooled to manufacture the Model A.

It is true that religion and philosophy and art do not "progress" in the same way that automotive design does. Religion and philosophy and art are in some way timeless, with a good anecdote from some thinker or other proving to be just the ticket for grappling with a contemporary issue. The human need for meaning and purpose remains. Nevertheless, it changes as we adjust to new realities.

The Model T demonstrated the need for paved roads. The multiplicity of human cultures in our shrinking world demands that we build religions and philosophies that will be positive—be roads and bridges, not muddy ditches.

The Bigness of Our Littleness

Francis Bacon—credited as the codifier of the scientific method—said that our knowledge suffers "from littleness of spirit and the smallness and slightness of the tasks which human industry has proposed to itself. And what is worst of all, this very littleness of spirit comes with a certain air of arrogance and superiority."

Some things never change!

In like manner, religious and philosophic thinking must not stick with past success. Revelation is—and must be—continuous.

Astrophysicist and science popularizer Neil deGrasse Tyson articulates the scientific method this way:

> Test ideas by experiment and observation.
> Build on those ideas that pass the test; reject those that fail.
> Follow the evidence wherever it leads.
> Question everything.[1]

Religion and art profit as much as science and automotive design by proceeding in this manner. For me, the scientific method is the ultimate spiritual practice. It clarifies and focuses the mind. It helps us find meaning and purpose on a human scale and something beneficial to human well-being.

For those of us concerned with helping others find meaning and purpose in an ever-changing world, however, the spiritual practice of the scientific methods helps us get on down the road.

The same can be said of those who do not follow the scientific method as a way of sussing out the best approximations of reality. The scientific method represents the closest approximation to the way things are that can be found by human beings. I say this as a poet and a member of the clergy, two fields that have not traditionally given science pride of place when it comes to discovering reality.

---

1. From Braga and Druran, "Unafraid of the Dark."

What's the Humanist Mission?

As far as I'm concerned, there is no argument between science and religion—or poetry, come to that. Science is more likely to communicate a close approximation of what there is in the universe (and in our minds) than is religion or art. Religion and art are subjectivities. They are subjectivities that certainly can enthrall and inspire individuals and even large groups of people, perhaps even the entirety of humanity. Yet, they remain subjectivities.

Is subjectivity "bad"? Of course not! It is where all of us live from day to day for most of our lives. Still, when we wish to come out of our personal caves, science offers the best method for approximating what is there.

Perhaps, as Ludwig Wittgenstein proposed, "The world is that which is the case," yet we do not, nor will we ever, know the case. The world and the case are, as Buddhists have long said, mirrors reflecting mirrors reflecting mirrors.

On Chopping Wood and Getting Unstuck

I was recently reminded of an old saw from my youth: "Anybody can cut wood after the tree is down." I long assumed that was an old bit of folk wisdom until I read a version of it in the work of Publilius Syrus, who was a Syrian slave in Italy (died 29 BCE).

Anybody can cut wood after the tree is down. The saying is about those intrepid people who do the initial work, the hard cutting that makes life easier for others.

Somebody's got to do it, as the cliché goes.

In his book *A Failure of Nerve: Leadership in the Age of the Quick Fix*, Rabbi Ed Friedman lists three characteristics of what he calls an "imaginatively gridlocked society": a treadmill of always trying harder, a focus on finding answers rather than reframing questions, and a polarization into false dichotomies."

Those are very fine ideas for problem-solving in organizations. They are also excellent for problem-solving in our lives . . . and every day presents a problem, doesn't it?

When we get stuck in our own stuff, that's exactly what we've done: jumped on a treadmill of always trying harder, focused on finding answers rather than reframing questions, and fallen into "false dichotomies"—black-and-white, either/or thinking.

It is the stuff of political discourse and the self-help industry.

When we jump on that treadmill of always trying harder and focus on finding answers by using to old saws of false dichotomies, we are cutting wood but not cutting down the tree.

This sort of getting stuck isn't so much a failure of nerve as it is an abrogation of our own power. "Would you have a great empire? Rule over yourself," said Stoic philosopher Publius Syrus.[1]

---

1. Publius Syrus, *Moral Sayings*.

The Olympics of a Reflective Life

I often find it best to start out by stating the obvious, and this is what I think is obvious, anyway, about those of us who choose our philosophy or religious tradition: we pick one (or pick elements of various ones) because we find its suggested practices and commitments useful in constructing the formula for a good life.

I think I've got that right.

Consequently, having pre-chosen a life-stance, we are better able to deal with life's inevitable highs and lows. We have a method!

As for me, a style of Christianity was chosen for me at birth due to the circumstances and geography of my birth. My experience of life, however, led me to question the meaning, methods, and efficacy of the style of Christianity that my birth had chosen for me.

First I questioned that form of Christianity, then I questioned Christianity itself. For me, Christianity did not offer answers to the questions that I felt were getting asked as I lived my life.

For those lucky enough to get a choice, the criteria for choosing a new philosophy or religion (or, gosh help us, a "spirituality") would appear to be something that makes sense and creates meaning and purpose in our lives.

As a humanist, I'm partial to that earlier humanistic philosophy, Stoicism, and for my money the Stoic philosopher Epictetus (died 135 CE) said it best in chapter 29 of his *Enchiridion,* or "Manual":

> In all things, think about
> what comes before
> and what comes after.
>
> Then, act. Otherwise,
> you will start with a bang
> and then begin to whimper.
>
> Who doesn't want to be

After the Bloody Mary Game

an Olympic champion?

But give some thought to
what comes before the glory
and what comes after.

If you want all of it—
the rules,
the diet,
the exercise—
go for it. Make your
trainer your boss.

Want to be a gladiator?
You might get slammed;
you might eat dust;
you might get beaten.

Think about it.

If you still want it,
go for it. But first,
consider—or you will look
like the kids who play at
wrestler or gladiator.

Consider or, like an ape,
you will mimic what you see,
then wander to the next thing.

Consider. Go for what
you want with zeal.

Want to be a philosopher?
It's not all about the talking.

Consider: What do you want?
Want to be a wrestler?

What's the Humanist Mission?

> Do you have the back for it, the legs?
>
> We all have different strengths.
> Stoics don't gorge,
> don't get angry, don't get drunk.
> They follow a middle way.
>
> Consider all this, then,
> go ahead, if you want.
> But be consistent.
>
> Either act with integrity
> or look like a child at play.
>
> Cultivate your reason;
> cultivate your body.
> Work on your inside and
> your outside.
>
> Do some thinking about it.
> Or be one of the mob. (author's translation)

Epictetus gets at that central problem with potential: we can want in several different directions and end up playing lots of parts but never achieving anything.

The mere fact that many human beings alive today have the choice of which religions and philosophies to follow can lead to lots of sampling and very little savoring. We must remember the point of religions and philosophies: to aid us in achieving meaning and purpose, "the good life."

What was true in the Rome of Epictetus is true today: You can't be an Olympic wrestler, gladiator, and philosopher, except in virtual reality. In this we reality, we all must choose where our priorities lie. Religions and philosophies offer sets of practices and commitments that—ideally, anyway—help with those choices.

After thanking your lucky stars for the freedom to choose, do some thinking about it. As Epictetus would say:

> Consider. Go for what
> you want with zeal.

The Ol' Heave-Ho-Ho

You've seen them spilling off the paved trail into the woods; you've seen them in parks, across sand dunes, wherever people go. There's no standard English phrase for them. A couple of terms are "desire paths" and "goat trails." In another era, they were called "bootleg trails." They are those paths that steadfastly ignore the "Keep to the Trail" or "Keep Off the Grass" signs and dart off on their own, wearing paths of least resistance or of the shortest distance between two points.

Desire paths. Sometimes planners give up and pave them; sometimes fences go up that are promptly trampled down. If there's one thing we human beings are good at, it's finding the quickest way to our desires—they aren't called "goat trails" for nothin'. Sure, they look like the paths goats make; they also serve to get us to our desires faster, as we follow the goat-footed god Pan, often in the word inspired by his name, "panic."

Religions have served a public and personal good through the millennia, sometimes erecting fences across desire paths (that quickly get trampled down), sometimes creating new desire paths (such as martyrdom or saintliness), and sometimes explaining unavoidable desire paths as the will of one god or another.

Ours is not the first human generation to want everything now, now, now. A whole folk wisdom tradition has arisen around advice to postpone desires—"If wishes were horses," the old saying goes, "beggars would ride."

Everyone knows that "good things come to those who wait." Many of us have felt the sorrow summed up in "a minute on the lips, forever on the hips."

And, perhaps my favorite, "early ripe, early rotten."

British behavioral scientist Paul Dolan recently published a book called *Happiness by Design*. The subtitle is *Change What You Do, Not What You Think*. Dolan makes some excellent points: We are what we pay attention to. Forgot about what a person believes, or wishes for; look for what someone actually does.

What's the Humanist Mission?

Look at your "to do" list. What are you actually excited about doing on that list? That's where your attention is going to go. Look at the desire path you are taking to get there.

Attention is a limited resource: put it one place, and it necessarily isn't in another place. And sometimes it can be nowhere at all.

There's a great deal of talk these days about "mindfulness," which is a method by which we can notice where our attention is going.

The opposite of mindfulness is mind-less-ness. Autopilot. That's when you think about how you got somewhere and realize that you can't remember the trip. That's when you're way down a desire path before realizing it's a pointless trip.

Bertrand Russell perhaps summed it up best: "To be without some of the things you want is an indispensable part of happiness."

What am I doing because I'm "supposed to be" doing it? What am I doing because I've always done it? Where am I putting my attention? I'm sitting down, looking around, and thinking about it. Because, as the sacred scripture of Led Zeppelin tells us, "There's still time to change the road you're on."

Going All Thoreau:
Doing Social Justice

Let's consider an extreme example, a stark instance of the decision between doing something and talking about it. The abolitionist John Brown, fed up with the endless wrangling and political maneuvering over slavery in the early nineteenth century, decided to take matters into his own hands. He led a group that attacked a US military arsenal with the intention of seizing the weapons—Sharps rifles, which were a state-of-the-art weapon of the time—and arming slaves. Brown was captured and, in the case of the State of Virginia versus John Brown, charged with murder, incitement to riot, and treason. Brown was hanged for his actions.

But that's not the action I want to consider.

One of the financial contributors to John Brown's violent plan was Henry David Thoreau. Nowadays Thoreau's reputation is mostly as an individualist and a naturalist. But in his own time, he was seen by many as a fiery abolitionist and as an anarchist.

There was never any doubt that John Brown would be convicted and hanged. The debated question—and it is still alive in American popular culture—is whether or not John Brown was crazy. (Look at the pictures and portraits of Brown sometime to see what I mean.)

Slavery sympathizers insisted that Brown had to be crazy: no White man in his right mind would arm slaves. Abolitionists, on the other hand, insisted that the horror of slavery had driven Brown to this extremity, and that the longer slavery existed, the more Browns there would be. Thoreau went on a lecture tour in support of this view, presenting everywhere he could a lecture that became an essay called "A Plea for Captain John Brown." There Thoreau says,

> I do not think it is quite sane for one to spend his whole life in talking or writing about this matter, unless he is continuously inspired, and I have not done so. A man may have other affairs to attend to. I do not wish to kill nor to be killed, but I can foresee circumstances in which both these things would be by me unavoidable. We

preserve the so-called peace of our community by deeds of petty violence every day. Look at the policeman's billy and handcuffs! Look at the jail! Look at the gallows! Look at the chaplain of the regiment! We are hoping only to live safely on the outskirts of this provisional army. So we defend ourselves and our hen-roosts, and maintain slavery. I know that the mass of my countrymen think that the only righteous use that can be made of Sharps rifles and revolvers is to fight duels with them, when we are insulted by other nations, or to hunt Indians, or shoot fugitive slaves with them, or the like. I think that for once the Sharps rifles and the revolvers were employed in a righteous cause. The tools were in the hands of one who could use them.

Dangerous words in 1859. Thoreau the anarchist appears in these lines:

The only government that I recognize—and it matters not how few are at the head of it, or how small its army—is that power that establishes justice in the land, never that which establishes injustice. What shall we think of a government to which all the truly brave and just men in the land are enemies, standing between it and those whom it oppresses? A government that pretends to be Christian and crucifies a million Christs every day!

Clearly, Thoreau believed that working for justice includes direct action and taking to the street.

While the John Brown affair clearly energized Thoreau, it put his friend and supporter Ralph Waldo Emerson in a bind. Though Emerson was a leading progressive intellectual at the time, and a friend or acquaintance of most of the leading abolitionists, he had been very careful in his words about the abolition of slavery. Emerson did not put much faith in political solutions. Or politics, for that matter.

When news of the capture of John Brown reached him, Emerson wrote to his son, "We are all very well, in spite of the sad Harper's Ferry business, which interests us all who had Brown for our guest twice. . . . He is a true hero, but lost his head there."

No, neither Emerson nor Thoreau thought much of governments in general or of democracy. They were individualists and elitists. Emerson once said, "Democracy becomes a government of bullies tempered by editors." He might nowadays rephrase that as, "Democracy becomes a government of bullies manipulated by media."

The question was what to do about it. Thoreau said to take direct action; Emerson said to sit back and think about it—what we might call the "pen is mightier than the sword" approach. These two had a clear choice: Contemplative or activist? Scholar or reformer? Bomb thrower or navel-gazer?

This tension has long plagued religions and the religious. Here's what Thoreau thought about that, speaking of John Brown:

> This man was an exception, for he did not set up even a political graven image between him and his God.
>
> A church that can never have done with excommunicating Christ while it exists! Away with your broad and flat churches, and your narrow and tall churches! Take a step forward, and invent a new style of out-houses. Invent a salt that will save you, and defend our nostrils.
>
> The modern Christian is a man who has consented to say all the prayers in the liturgy, provided you will let him go straight to bed and sleep quietly afterward. All his prayers begin with "Now I lay me down to sleep," and he is forever looking forward to the time when he shall go to his "long rest."

Henry, Henry, that's not nice! Comparing the contents of churches with the contents of outhouses? Not nice at all! But can't you hear the indignation with navel-gazing?

Emerson and Thoreau are good examples of the antipodes, the opposites, of those who think and those who do. Consider: Emerson and Thoreau lived before psychoanalysis. The word "narcissism" wasn't coined until 1899. Emerson and Thoreau never heard the term "mental health." Or "introvert" or "extrovert." But Thoreau knew he had to get outside his own stuff—that he had to stop navel-gazing—and get to work saving the lives of those Americans who were suffering injustice.

It's easy to think Thoreau was right all along, now that we know how it all worked out. Thoreau didn't live to see how it all worked out. He died in 1862. He never had a chance to put his values to the test in the war. He never saw slavery abolished.

In that way, Thoreau was like the rest of us: we may never see the outcome of our struggles for justice. Thoreau is here to remind us that that is not an excuse.

Conscience and Choosing the Hill to Die On

During the Ebola scare of 2015 I watched the case of Maine nurse Kaci Hickox closely. She was under house arrest for her refusal to obey regulations she considered silly. Eventually, a federal judge released her. In my mind, anyway, Kaci Hickox is a hero for her resistance to fear-based, anti-scientific, and politically motivated quarantine.

In 2012 the US military experienced an odd occurrence: for the first time in US history during a time of war, more active duty troops died due to suicide than to combat.

Chinese human rights lawyer Gao Zhiseng disappeared in 2009. He reappeared in 2015, in prison, with no charges against him and no release date.

Shirin Ebadi, an Iranian lawyer, risked torture, imprisonment, and death fighting in the courts for the rights of women and children in Iran.

All these people stepped out of line. They disobeyed their governments. Some disobeyed the dictates of their religions. Most are disliked by most their fellow citizens. Some of them chose death rather than a life of guilt and shame.

Why do people do things that sometimes get them killed, sometimes imprisoned, sometimes demoted or fired or exposed to the scorn of millions of their fellow citizens?

What drives all of this crazy, counterintuitive behavior? Conscience. And the mental punishment inflicted by conscience, guilt. Conscience. The feeling that some actions cannot be condoned, no matter how "legal" they are. The feeling that enables we human beings to take actions for the good of others rather than at the expense of ourselves.

Why do human beings have a conscience? Isn't a conscience merely a drag on getting ahead? Henry David Thoreau said in his handbook for rebellion, the essay "Civil Disobedience," "If the machine of government is of such a nature that it requires you to be the agent of injustice to another, then, I say, break the law."

Even though Thoreau's thoughts have become the template for those acting on conscience, notice that word "machine." Thoreau saw conscience as an individual attribute against a deterministic mass. But it isn't always, is it? Sometimes, as in the case of Edward Snowden, the machine is ambiguous.

We still don't know why *Homo sapiens sapiens*—the "wise man," as scientists have (perhaps overconfidently) called our species—began to have a conscience. My vote for best hypothesis goes to British anthropologist Robin Dunbar.

Dunbar theorizes that human language developed as a result of the need to socially interact in larger groups. Neanderthal, for example—also known as *Homo sapiens neanderthalensis*—traveled in very small bands and were for the most part inbred. They didn't use a whole lot a gray matter figuring out what other people were thinking or trying to get along with an extended group. They didn't use their words much, and so didn't have a need for a great many. They probably didn't have much of a conscience, either.

Navigating the deep and often stormy waters of multiple relationships, however, required a good many words and concepts. And this may be why the children of *Homo sapiens sapiens* developed complex language. It was a matter of talking about it or dying. It was also a matter of considering multiple goods in the gray shades that human existence swims in.

Emotions are in the gut. But it takes gray matter and complex language to make the complex decisions a Solomon . . . or you . . . have to make.

Philosopher Peter Singer says there are two types of conscience: the traditional and the critical. This goes some way into an important distinction. Most people have that traditional form of conscience. It's the stuff of traditional religions. It's the level of confidence in others that allows us to work in offices and live in communities. Almost all human beings have it.

The people who get the Nobel Peace Prize are of the critical variety. A Malala or Shirin Ebadi. They have considered the arguments of the majority. They have heard the arguments of traditional religion. And they have decided to act for a greater good.

The right thing to do isn't always clear. Human governments aren't faceless machines of conformity, as Thoreau appears to have thought. The individual isn't always correct. (The deluded decision-making of Timothy McVeigh demonstrates that point.) Yet, *Homo sapiens sapiens* gets wiser only though the actions of brave individuals risking themselves and thinking way outside the box.

It is that accumulation of brave thinkers that may, someday, make us truly wise.

Eleanor Rigby's Selfie

We learned from the Beatles that Eleanor Rigby "keeps her face in a jar by the door." Clearly the Fab Four thought that was not a good thing to do. But what were they critiquing? Was it where Eleanor kept her face? Or that she had a "face to meet the faces that we meet" at all? Should we wear the same face all the time? Is one of our faces the "true" one?

Whether or not there's noise when a tree falls in the forest, a more pertinent question for us is whether or not we have a face, a personality, when no one is around to experience it. Therefore, Eleanor Rigby's plight haunts us still. We know she's out there. We don't want to become her. We fear that she is faceless. We fear that for ourselves. Most of us wish perhaps that we were like the stone imagined by Emily Dickinson:

> How happy is the little Stone
> That rambles in the Road alone,
> And doesn't care about Careers
> And Exigencies never fears—

Perhaps we wish to be ". . . independent as the Sun." In our hearts, however, we know very well that we are creatures dependent upon others of our kind. And that's scary.

In the nineteenth century, US prisons adopted the practice of solitary confinement, depriving a prisoner of visual stimulation and human contact. At the time, the idea was that a prisoner with some "alone time" would reflect on his or her misdeeds and come out a better person. It was quickly noticed, however, that instead of becoming moral paragons, prisoners in solitary confinement began to exhibit symptoms of mental illness.

After this discovery, the practice was for the most part discontinued until the late twentieth century, when US prisons began to transition from a rehabilitation model to one of retribution. Now we know that being alone hurts . . . a lot. And that's why prisons do it. (There are in the US today something on the order of 80,000 prisoners in solitary confinement at any given time.)

Sure, introverts such as myself need some time alone, with faces in the jar, to process what we experience in the hustle and bustle of those loud extroverts. But people—even introverts—don't like being alone for extended periods. It drives us crazy. Therefore, when we are alone, those of us not under arrest find ways to simulate human interaction—TV, social media, perhaps even writing a letter. We are social creatures. We need human interaction. We need an excuse to put our faces on.

After my father died, my mother found herself alone after sixty-five years of companionship. She wondered aloud: Should she give up and leave her face in the jar by the door? Was it disloyal of her not to do so? She no longer felt like Emily Dickinson's independent little stone. She felt the full weight of dependency.

My prescription for my mother (and Eleanor Rigby) is ... go to church! Or bowling. Or a book club. Something. Father McKenzie's message (or disconnected ramblings about a book) may not be much to text home about, but the coffee, wine, or potluck involved might just be the ticket.

A member of my congregation recently brought me one of those graphics called a "bubble cloud," generated by a questionnaire concerning what was important to a Christian congregation near my humanist congregation. The most-used word? "Community." And the congregation I serve would have the same big bubble, "Community." In their case, "Christ," and in our case, "reason," would be tiny little bubbles compared with the true reason we gather as congregations—community.

Human interaction reminds us to pull our faces out of that jar.

As the Beatles knew, denizens of post-industrial countries may exist in utter isolation. We often shop in anonymous supermarkets rather than bustling markets. We buy clothing off a hanger, not from the source of the craft. As Robert D. Putnam pointed out, many of us "bowl alone."

I don't think any of us has an "authentic" or "true" face. We adjust the faces we pull from the jar according to the circumstances of our interactions. We have a "going to a funeral" face, a "going to the theater" face, and so on. These are constructed in the bustle of human relationships. Without the bustle, we don't bother. And that's not good for us.

Perhaps Eleanor—and all the lonely people—should share a selfie. Not a bad first step in getting that face out of the jar by the door and spiffed up a bit. Then? Go to church. Or temple or mosque or ... a bowling team. Perhaps even chat with Father McKenzie. Who knows what he knows when he's not pontificating ...

A Final Summary of Humanism:
Who We Are, What We Do, Why It Matters

Who We Are

Religions and philosophies serve as heuristic devices for life, providing shape and meaning to what otherwise may seem a shapeless, chaotic rush. For some, religious views are chosen by birth or circumstance; for others religions are a matter of passing indifference in the rush toward the goals of a given social order.

Some people—a fortunate few—both *have* the chance and *take* the chance to consider which heuristic device is best for them in pursuing meaning and purpose in life.

Some choose humanism as a way of being and a way of life.

Humanism has grown up. It is past the polemics common to new belief systems. Humanism's existence is established, its voice clear. Those who wish to live an ethical life based on reason, the humanities, and evidence will find humanism if they search. Humanists choose to live a meaningful, purposeful life, consciously and ethically, outside of conventional religious traditions.

The dream and opportunity of humanism is the dream and opportunity for a responsible and purposeful life. A life free of the fears that have haunted the human mind for so long. Humanism is freedom—the freedom to realize that the old demons of the human mind are mere chimeras. The freedom to live in the world of the real and the possible.

Humanists realize that it matters what one thinks is right and wrong with the world. The humanist life stance is clear concerning our commitments: political and legal equity for all, preferential treatment for the historically marginalized, freedom *of* religion and *from* religion, the separation of the public and private spheres. Compassion, acceptance, equity.

What We Do

In constructing our life stance, many humanists attempt to live up to what the Stoics called a rational nature. The path to a rational nature includes these guides:

1. Do not give assent either to what is false or to what is unclear.
2. Act only in ways that serve the human community and the planet.
3. Joyfully greet that which is of the nature of the universe.

As Roman emperor and philosopher Marcus Aurelius phrased the way to a rational nature, "Wipe away your illusions. Control your inclinations. Extinguish your desires. Control your will." Another way of saying this: "To what should we give serious attention? Just intentions; social actions; telling the truth; and a disposition joyfully accepting the nature of the cosmos."[1]

Admittedly, the Stoics of old sought two universals that we now know do not exist: universal reason (*logos*) and cosmic purpose (*teleos*). Still, the Stoics and Epicureans and others of pre-Christian thinking offer usable alternatives for a post-Christian worldview. After all, there are two very different worldviews: to disdain the nature of this existence, naming it tedious and transitory; or to commit to it as the only life we know. Disdain or commitment? This is a central question for each of us.

Consider what leaps to mind when you hear the phrase "spiritual practice"—prayer perhaps, scripture reading perhaps, or some form of meditation. This is imagination driven by the influence of Christianity on the Western mind, but humanists attempt to pick up the pieces left after the Christian dominance. (The Latin word *meditatio* meant everything from study to practice to habit.) It is perhaps surprising that, before Christianity, the Stoics considered "applied physics" a spiritual discipline. So was the contemplation of logic and ethics.

Why? Because physics reveals the nature of the reality we live in and are part of. The Stoics thought that adjusting to the reality of what is is in itself a virtue, and the only cure for the anguish inherent in the human condition. A philosophical life centers on the realization that the world around us is not a means to an end. It merely *is*. From this, using logic, flows our ethical stances. "Ethics" in this context means doing that which is good. Meditation on physics, logic, and ethics leads to adjustments in our way of

---

1. *Meditations*, IX.7; IV.33 (author's translation).

being each day, which is the point of living a philosophical life, whose goal is that rarest of human gifts: wisdom.

Why It Matters

Humanism is not the contemplation of the perfect human action—WWJD ("What Would Jesus Do?")—but rather the contemplation of human action within the context of the cosmos itself—WDCR ("What *Does* the Cosmos Require?").

We know, for example, that human beings evolved as prosocial creatures in tribal circumstances. This tells us much about human behavior and how we act toward each other. The ethics codified in religious systems are in truth evolved prosocial traits. A conscious knowledge of this fact helps in understanding how to hone and increase our prosocial traits, our ethics.

Here is a humanist heuristic for life: If this is our only precious life, then it is up to us, isn't it? First, to love what happens, or at the least to have the strength to grin and bear its punch when tragedy strikes. Second, to wring from existence all the joy life may provide and share it with as much of the world as we can. Third, to make this world a better place, now and in the future, for the sake of the planet and all conscious beings.

Humanism matters because life, here and now, matters. (Many of these ideas are better stated in *Philosophy as a Way of Life*, by Pierre Hadot.)

Conclusion
Again Play the Bloody Mary Game

1. Go into a windowless bathroom and close the door.
2. Light a candle.
3. Turn off the electric light.
4. Turn on the water, hot or cold.
5. Spin around three times, saying, "I killed your baby, Mary Worth! I killed your baby, Mary Worth! I killed your baby, Mary Worth!"
6. Look into the mirror. Really, closely, look into the mirror.
7. Think of all the stories human beings have told. So many of them are frightening. A little candle light, a few rhythmic words—why do we get frightened?

Why indeed.

Sources and Further Reading

Allport, Gordon. *The Nature of Prejudice: 25th Anniversary Edition*. Boston: Perseus, 1979.
Ames, Roger T., and David L. Hall. *Daodejing: "Making This Life Significant": A Philosophical Translation*. New York: Ballantine, 2004.
Ardrey, Robert. *African Genesis: A Personal Investigation into the Animal Origins and Nature of Man*. New York: Atheneum, 1961.
Ariely, Dan. *Predictably Irrational: The Hidden Forces That Shape Our Decisions*. New York: Harper Perennial, 2008.
Asad, Talal. *Formations of the Secular: Christianity, Islam, Modernity*. Stanford, CA: Stanford University Press, 2003.
Bacon, Francis. *The Essays*. New York: Penguin Classics, 1986.
Batson, C. Daniel. *The Altruism Question: Toward a Social-Psychological Answer*. New York: Psychology, 1991.
Bénabou, Roland, David Ticci, and Andrea Vindigni. "Forbidden Fruits: The Political Economy of Science, Religion, and Growth." NBER Working Paper 21105. April 2015. http://www.nber.org/papers/w21105.
Bernays, Edward. *Propaganda*. Brooklyn, NY: Ig, 2005.
Black's Law Dictionary. Bryan A. Garner, editor in chief. 3rd ed. Eagan, MN: Thomson West, 2006.
Bok, Sissela. *Exploring Happiness: From Aristotle to Brain Science*. New Haven, CT: Yale University Press, 2010.
Braga, Brannon, and Ann Druran, writers and directors. "Unafraid of the Dark." *Cosmos: A Spacetime Odyssey*, episode 13. National Geographic Channel, June 8, 2014.
Brecht, Bertolt. *Selected Poems*. Translated by H. R. Hays. New York: Harvest, 1971.
Breeden, David, Wally Swist, and Steven Schroeder, translators. *Daodejing*. Beaumont, TX: Lamar University Press, 2015.
Brooks, David. *The Road to Character*. New York: Random House, 2015
Carson, Rachael. *Silent Spring*. Boston: Mariner, 2002.
Cave, Peter. *Humanism: A Beginner's Guide*. Oxford: OneWorld, 2009.
Chapman, Gary. *The Five Love Languages: How to Express Heartfelt Commitment to Your Mate*. Chicago: Northfield: 2004.
Churchill, Winston. *The Power of Words*. Edited by Martin Gilbert. Boston: De Capo, 2012.
Churchland, Patricia S. *Touching a Nerve: The Self as Brain*. New York: Norton, 2013.
Clarke, James Freeman. *Manual of Unitarian Belief*. Boston: Unitarian Sunday School Society, 1890. https://babel.hathitrust.org/cgi/pt?id=hvd.ah21au;view=1up;seq=5.
Clements, Jonathan. *Darwin's Notebook: The Life, Times, and Discoveries of Charles Robert Darwin*. Philadelphia: Running Press, 2009.

Sources and Further Reading

Comte, August. *Auguste Comte and Positivism: The Essential Writings.* Edited by Gertrud Lenzer. New York: Harper & Row, 1975.
Csikszentmihalyi, Mihaly. *Flow: The Psychology of Optimal Experience.* New York: HarperCollins, 1991.
"The Curious Case of Mary Toft." University of Glasgow Library Special Collections Department. Book of the Month, August 2009. http://special.lib.gla.ac.uk/exhibns/month/aug2009.html.
Dalai Lama XIV, Desmond Tutu, and Douglas Carlton Abrams. *The Book of Joy: Lasting Happiness in a Changing World.* New York: Avery, 2016.
Darwin, Charles. *The Life and Letters of Charles Darwin.* Vol. 1. Edited by Francis Darwin. New York: Wallachia, 2015.
Dawkins, Richard. *The Selfish Gene.* Oxford: Oxford University Press, 1976.
De Botton, Alain. *Religion for Atheists: A Non-Believers Guide to the Uses of Religion.* New York: Pantheon, 2012.
De Waal, Frans. *The Bonobo and the Atheist: In Search of Humanism among the Primates.* New York: Norton, 2013.
Dewey, John. *Art as Experience.* New York: Capricorn, 1958.
Dickens, Charles. *Nicholas Nickleby.* New York: Penguin Classics, 1999.
Dickinson, Emily. *The Complete Poems of Emily Dickinson.* Edited by Thomas H. Johnson. Boston: Little, Brown, 1960.
Didion, Joan. *We Tell Ourselves Stories in Order to Live: Collected Nonfiction.* New York: Everyman's Library, 2003.
Dietrich, John. First Unitarian Society of Minneapolis Archives. http://www.firstunitarian.org/FUSArchives/.
Diogenes. *Early Greek Philosophy.* Translated by Jonathan Barnes. New York: Penguin, 2001.
Dolan, Paul. *Happiness by Design: Finding Pleasure and Purpose in Everyday Life.* New York: Plume, 2014.
Dostoyevsky, Fyodor. *The Brothers Karamazov.* Translated by Constance Garnett. Mineola, NY: Dover, 2005.
Dowd, Michael. *Thank God for Evolution: How the Marriage of Science and Religion Will Transform Your Life and Our World.* New York: Viking, 2008.
Eagleton, Terry. *The Meaning of Life: A Very Short Introduction.* New York: Oxford University Press, 2008.
Eliot, George. *The Essays of George Eliot.* Edited by Nathan Sheppard. New York: Funk & Wagnalls, 2013.
Emerson, Ralph Waldo. *Poems.* New York: Everyman's Library, 2004.
Epictetus, *Enchiridion.* Translated by P. E. Matheson. http://www.sacred-texts.com/cla/dep/index.htm.
Epicurus. *The Art of Happiness.* Translated by George K. Strodach. New York: Penguin, 2012.
Ericson, Edward L. *The Humanist Way: An Introduction to Ethical Humanist Religion.* New York: Continuum, 1988.
Finnigan, Mary. "Mingyur Rinpoche, the Millionaire Monk Who Renounced It All." *The Guardian,* September 22, 2011.
Flaherty, Joseph. "'Godfather of the Dead; George A. Romero Talks Zombies." *Wired,* June 2010. https://www.wired.com/2010/06/george-a-romero-zombies/.
Friedman, Edward H. *A Failure of Nerve: Leadership in the Age of the Quick Fix.* New York: Church Publishing, 2007.

Sources and Further Reading

Fuller, Margaret. *The Essential Margaret Fuller*. Edited by Martin Gilbert. Princeton, NJ: Rutgers University Press, 1992.

Gardner, John. *Moral Fiction*. New York: Basic Books, 1979.

Gay, Peter. *The Enlightenment: An Interpretation*. Vol. 1, *The Rise of Modern Paganism*. New York: Norton, 1995.

Gendler, Tamar Szabó. "Alief and Belief." *Journal of Philosophy* 5.10, Epistemic Norms, part 2 (October 2008) 634–63. http://www.jstor.org/stable/20620132.

Ginsberg, Allen. *Collected Poems 1947–1980*. San Francisco: City Lights, 1988.

Gioia, Dana. "Words." https://www.poets.org/poetsorg/poem/words.

Godin, Seth. *We Are All Weird: The Rise of Tribes and the End of Normal*. New York: Penguin, 2011.

Hadot, Pierre. *The Inner Citadel: The Meditations of Marcus Aurelius*. Translated by Michael Chase. Cambridge MA: Harvard University Press, 1998.

———. *What Is Ancient Philosophy?* Translated by Michael Chase. Cambridge, MA: Belknap Press of Harvard University Press, 2002.

Hardy, Thomas. *The Mayor of Casterbridge*. New York: Vintage Classics, 2016.

———. *Selected Poetry*. New York: Oxford University Press, 1996.

Harris, Mark W. *Elite: Uncovering Classism in Unitarian Universalist History*. Boston: Skinner House, 2011.

Harris, Sam. *The Moral Landscape: How Science Can Determine Human Values*. New York: Free Press, 2010.

Heath, Chip, and Dan Heath. *Made to Stick: Why Some Ideas Survive and Others Die*. New York: Random House, 2007.

Hecht, Jennifer Michael. *Doubt: A History: The Great Doubters and Their Legacy of Innovation, from Socrates and Jesus to Thomas Jefferson and Emily Dickinson*. New York: HarperCollins, 2003.

Heidegger Martin. *Basic Writings*. New York: HarperPerennial, 1993.

Henriques, Gregg. "Six Domains of Psychological Well-Being." *Psychology Today*, May 15, 2014. https://www.psychologytoday.com/blog/theory-knowledge/201405/six-domains-psychological-well-being.

Holmes, John Haynes. *Heros in Peace*. The 6th William Penn Lecture. Philadelphia: Walter H. Jenkins, 1920. http://www.gutenberg.org/ebooks/author/7713.

Honderich, Ted, ed. *The Oxford Companion to Philosophy*. New York: Oxford University Press, 1995.

Humanist Manifesto I, II, and III. American Humanist Association, 1933, 1973, 2003. https://americanhumanist.org/what-is-humanism/manifesto1/.

Huxley, T. H. "Agnosticism and Christianity." http://aleph0.clarku.edu/huxley/CE5/Agn-X.html.

James, William. *The Varieties of Religious Experience: A Study in Human Nature*. New York: Penguin, 1982.

Jefferson, Thomas. *Writings: Autobiography / Notes on the State of Virginia / Public and Private Papers / Addresses / Letters*. Edited by Merrill D. Peterson. New York: Library of America, 1984.

Jones, William R. *Is God a White Racist?: A Preamble to Black Theology*. Boston: Beacon, 1998.

Kaufman, Gordon D. *God the Problem*. Cambridge, MA: Harvard University Press, 1972.

———. *In Face of Mystery: A Constructive Theology*. Cambridge, MA: Harvard University Press, 1995.

Sources and Further Reading

Khaneman, Daniel. *Thinking, Fast and Slow*. New York: Farrar, Straus and Giroux, 2011.
Konnikova, Maria, "Why We Need Answers." *The New Yorker*, April 30, 2013.
Kramer, Roderick M. "Motivation and Emotion." *Organizational Behavior* 18.2 (June 1994) 199–230. https://www.gsb.stanford.edu/faculty-research/publications/sinister-attribution-error-paranoid-cognition-collective-distrust.
Krishnamurti, Jiddu. *Freedom from the Known*. New York: HarperCollins, 2009.
Kurtz, Paul. *The Humanist Alternative: Some Definitions of Humanism*. Buffalo, NY: Prometheus, 1973.
Lakoff, George, and Mark Johnson. *Philosophy in the Flesh: The Embodied Mind and Its Challenge to Western Thought*. New York: Basic, 1999.
Langer, Ellen J. *Mindfulness*. Cambridge, MA: Da Capo, 1989.
Le Poidevin, Robin. *Agnosticism: A Very Short Introduction*. New York: Oxford University Press, 2010.
Levant, Ronald F., Katherine Richmond, et al. "A Multicultural Investigation of Masculinity Ideology and Alexithymia." *Psychology of Men & Masculinity* 4.2 (July 2003) 91–99. https://www.researchgate.net/publication/232502554_A_Multicultural_Investigation_of_Masculinity_Ideology_and_Alexithymia.
Lincoln, Abraham. *Selected Speeches and Writings*. New York: Library of America, 1992.
Little, Charles. *Freedom Moves West: A History of the Western Unitarian Conference*. Boston: Beacon, 1952.
MacIntyre, Alasdair. *The MacIntyre Reader*. Edited by Kelvin Knight. Cambridge, UK: Polity, 1998.
Maitreya, Ananda, translator. *The Dhammapada*. Berkeley, CA: Parallax, 1995.
Marcus Aurelius. *Meditations: A New Translation*. Translated by Gregory Hays. New York: Modern Library, 2003.
May, Rollo. *The Courage to Create*. New York: Norton, 1994.
Mearns, Hugh. "Antigonish" https://www.poets.org/poetsorg/poem/antigonish-i-met-man-who-wasnt-there.
Menand, Louis, ed. *Pragmatism: A Reader*. New York: Vintage, 1997.
Merton, Thomas. *The Way of Chuang Tzu*. New York: New Directions, 1969.
Mitford, Jessica. *The American Way of Death Revisited*. New York: Vintage, 2000.
Mozi. *Basic Writings*. Translated by Burton Watson. New York: Columbia University Press, 1961.
The New Oxford Annotated Bible: New Revised Standard Version with the Apocrypha. Edited by Michael D. Coogan. New York: Oxford University Press, 2010.
Nin, Anais. *The Diary of Anais Nin*. Vol. 4, *1944–1947*. New York: Harcourt Brace Jovanovich, 1971.
Nussbaum, Martha. *Upheavals of Thought: The Intelligence of Emotions*. New York: Cambridge University Press, 2001.
Olds, Mason. *American Religious Humanism*. Hamden, CT: Fellowship of Religious Humanists, 1996.
Pinn, Anthony B. *The End of God Talk: An African American Humanist Theology*. New York: Oxford University Press, 2012.
Planck, Max. *Scientific Autobiography and Other Papers*. Translated by Frank Gaynor. New York: Philosophical Library, reissued 2007.
Plato. *The Republic*. Translated by Christopher Rowe. New York: Penguin, 2012.
———. *Phaedo*. Translated by David Gallop. New York: Oxford University Press, 2009.
———. *Select Dialogues of Plato*. Translated by Henry Cary. New York: Harper, 1890.

Sources and Further Reading

Publius Syrus. *The Moral Sayings of Publius Syrus, a Roman Slave.* Translated by Darius Lyman. New York: L. E. Bernard, 1856. https://archive.org/stream/moralsayingspub00lymagoog/moralsayingspub00lymagoog_djvu.txt.

Puett, Michael, and Christine Gross-Loh. *The Path: What Chinese Philosophers Can Teach Us About the Good Life.* New York: Simon & Schuster, 2016.

Putnam, Robert D. *Bowling Alone: The Collapse and Revival of American Community.* New York: Simon & Schuster, 2000.

Putnam, Robert D., and David E. Campbell. *American Grace: How Religion Divides and Unites Us.* New York: Simon & Schuster, 2010.

Quine, W. V., and J. S. Ullian. *The Web of Belief.* New York: Random House, 1978.

Radest, Howard. *Felix Adler: An Ethical Culture.* New York: Peter Lang, 1998.

Reese, Curtis. *Humanist Religion.* New York: Macmillan, 1931.

Reese, W. L., ed. *Dictionary of Philosophy and Religion: Eastern and Western Thought.* Atlantic Highlands, NJ: Humanities Press, 1980.

Reps, Paul, and Nyogen Senzaki, eds. *Zen Flesh, Zen Bones.* Boston: Tuttle, 1998.

Robertson, Donald. *Stoicism and the Art of Happiness.* London: Hodder & Stoughton, 2013.

Rorty, Richard. *Philosophy and Social Hope.* New York: Penguin, 1999.

Russell, Bertrand. *Why I Am Not a Christian, and Other Essays on Religion and Related Subjects.* New York: Simon & Schuster, 1967.

Sartre, Jean-Paul. *Existentialism Is a Humanism.* Translated by Carol Macomber. New Haven, CT: Yale University Press, 2007.

Sartwell, Crispin. *The Art of Living: Aesthetics of the Ordinary in World Spiritual Traditions.* New York: Wallachia, 2015.

The School of Life. "The Great Philosophers 10: Martin Heidegger." *The Philosopher's Mail.* https://thephilosophersmail.com/perspective/the-great-philosophers-10-martin-heigedder/.

Seneca. *The Stoic Philosophy of Seneca: Essays and Letters.* Translated by Moses Hadas. New York: Norton, 1968.

Schulz, William F. *Making the Manifesto: The Birth of Religious Humanism.* Boston: Skinner House, 2004.

Smith, Charles. *Jump Soul: New and Selected Poems.* New York: Norton, 2014.

Smith, Christian, with Melinda Lundquist Denton. *Soul Searching: The Religious and Spiritual Lives of American Teenagers.* New York: Oxford University Press, 2005.

Smith, Jonathan Z. *Imagining Religion: From Babylon to Jonestown.* Chicago: University of Chicago Press, 1988.

Solnit, Rebecca. *Men Explain Things to Me and Other Essays.* London: Granta, 2014.

Spiegelberg, Frederick. *The Religion of No-Religion.* Stanford, CA: J. L. Delkin, 1948.

Stevens, Wallace. *Collected Poetry and Prose.* New York: Library of America, 1997.

Taylor, Charles. *A Secular Age.* Cambridge, MA: Belknap Press of Harvard University Press, 2007.

Thoreau, Henry David. *Walden.* New York: Everyman's Library, 1993.

———. *Wild Apples & a Plea for Captain John Brown.* Rockville, MD: ARC Manor, 2007.

Tutu, Mpho. "What Is Ubuntu?" Video. Desmond Tutu Peace Foundation, April 29, 2015. http://www.tutufoundationusa.org/2015/04/29/what-is-ubuntu/.

Tyson, Neil deGrasse, Michael Abram Strauss, and J. Richard Gott. *Welcome to the Universe: An Astrophysical Tour.* Princeton, NJ: Princeton University Press, 2016.

Vernon, Mark. *Understanding Humanism.* Black Lick, OH: McGraw-Hill, 2010.

Victoroff, Jeff, and Arie W. Kruglanski, eds. *Psychology of Terrorism: Classic and Contemporary Insights*. New York: Psychology Press, 2009.

Vinciguerra, Robert. "Continued Observations on the Egonovism of American Society and Dialogs with Egonovists." *OpEd News*, October 31, 2013. http://www.opednews.com/articles/Continued-Observations-on-by-Rob-Vinciguerra-Atheism_Partisan-Religion_Religion-And-Spirituality_Religion-And-Values-131031-81.html.

Watson, Peter. *The Age of Atheists: How We Have Sought to Live Since the Death of God*. New York: Simon & Schuster, 2014.

Watts, Alan. *Does It Matter?: Essays on Man's Relation to Materiality*. New York: Pantheon, 1970.

Whitmarsh, Tim. *Battling the Gods: Atheism in the Ancient World*. New York: Knopf, 2015.

Wittgenstein, Ludwig. *Tractatus Logico-Philosophicus*. Translated by Charles Kay Ogden. Mineola, NY: Dover, 1999.

Wood, Graeme. "What ISIS Really Wants." *The Atlantic*, March 2015. https://www.theatlantic.com/magazine/archive/2015/03/what-isis-really-wants/384980/.

Wright, Conrad, ed. *Three Prophets of Religious Liberalism: Channing, Emerson, Parker*. Boston: Unitarian Universalist Association, 1986.

Wright, Robert. *The Moral Animal: the New Science of Evolutionary Psychology*. New York: Pantheon, 1994.

Xenophanes. *Early Greek Philosophy*. Translated by Jonathan Barnes. New York: Penguin, 2001.

Yong, Ed. "Justice Is Served, but More So after Lunch: How Food-Breaks Sway the Decisions of Judges. *Not Exactly Rocket Science* (blog), *Discover*, April 11, 2011. http://blogs.discovermagazine.com/notrocketscience/2011/04/11/justice-is-served-but-more-so-after-lunch-how-food-breaks-sway-the-decisions-of-judges/.

Zimmer, Carl. "The Secret Life of Bees: The World's Leading Expert on Bee Behavior Discovers the Secrets of Decision-Making in a Swarm." *Smithsonian*, March 2012. http://www.smithsonianmag.com/science-nature/the-secret-life-of-bees-99559587/.

Zuckerman, Phil. *Living the Secular Life: New Answers to Old Questions*. New York: Penguin, 2015.

About the Author

The Rev. Dr. David Breeden is Senior Minister at First Unitarian Society of Minneapolis. He has a Master of Fine Arts in poetry from the Iowa Writers' Workshop and a PhD from the Center for Writers at the University of Southern Mississippi, with additional study in writing and Buddhism at Naropa Institute in Boulder, Colorado. He also has a Master of Divinity from Meadville Lombard Theological School.

Breeden has published four novels and fourteen books of poetry, the latest titled *Deep Fragrance (in the Valley of the Void)*. His book *Raging for the Exit: A Commonplace Book* is a correspondence in poetry with philosopher and theologian Steven Schroeder. His translation of the Daodejing is available from Lamar University Press.

Breeden is Dean of the Humanist Institute, President of the UU Humanist Association, and on the advisory board for Unitarian Universalists for a Just Economic Community. He is a member of the freedom-to-write group PEN Center USA.

David writes for UU Quest for Meaning, a blog on patheos.com. His personal blog is wayofoneness.com. He tweets at @DBreeden.